The Prosperity Code

Tatjana Valujeva

Clink Street

Published by Clink Street Publishing 2021

Copyright © 2021

First edition.

The author asserts the moral right under the Copyright, Designs and Patents Act 1988 to be identified as the author of this work.

ISBN:
978-1-913962-58-6 - paperback
978-1-913962-59-3 - ebook

Contents

Working with beliefs using Instant Transformation Technique   107

How to get rich and not die trying   133

Acknowledgements

I want to express my gratitude to the wonderful people who chose to be part of my game.

My parents and family were always supportive and helped me every step of my way. My cousins were the first who believed in my business sense. My friends helped to bring more fun into my life. My teachers at school and in life, a big thank you to you, too!

Simon and Darren, my supportive and loving partners – I could not have done it without you.

David Verdesi and Vianna Stybal – thank you for opening a whole new world for me. Thank you to the world's greatest motivational speakers who were there at the turning point in my life: Tony Robbins, Brian Tracy, Robert Kiyosaki, Jay Abraham and Darren Winters. Thank you to Nadia Vecher – it was you who inspired me to write this course and this book. My kids, you are so wise – I am in awe.

The Creator Of All That Is – my true inspiration, source of knowledge, and discoveries that I made and am sharing with you here.

Love you all.

Tatjana
London, 2020

A story about money

There's a famous story about a conversation between a young boy and a very rich old man.

The young boy asked this very rich old man how he made his fortune. The old man looked at the young boy and started telling his story.

"Well, it was in the depth of America's Great Depression, 1929," he said. "Poverty was everywhere. It was so bad I was down to my last nickel. So I had an idea to sell apples on a stand.

"With my last nickel, I bought some apples. I spent the entire day polishing them and making them look nice. I spent hours practising my sales pitch and working to sell the apples. I doubled my money.

"The very next day, I repeated the process and bought more apples. And, at the end of the day, I doubled my money again."

The young boy listened intently and chipped in, "Wow! Is that how you built your multimillion-dollar empire?"

And the man looked at him and smiled.

"Of course not," he chuckled. "Then my wife's auntie died and left us a fortune of $100 million dollars."

Introduction

"You're not on your own. And you know it all. You have already decided where to go, so trust yourself and enjoy the journey"

TATJANA VALUJEVA

What is The Prosperity Code?

The story you've just read about the rich old man and his fast track to wealth is a popular tale. It lays bare one of the most commonly held beliefs about money and wealth: that to become rich, you have to work hard or smart.

In this book, I will show you that making money is simple, easy, and fun. It is only our beliefs that hold us back from doing what we really want to do and getting what we really want.

This is *The Prosperity Code*. It's a way of understanding how wealth, health, and prosperity work, why you are the way you are, and how to change it.

I should know because I discovered the "secret" of *The Prosperity Code* in my journey to becoming a self-made millionaire and, most importantly, found my happiness. I moved from another country with nothing, tried lots of business ideas – some better than others as you'll find out – and succeeded.

My strong beliefs about money helped me get there. However, other beliefs led to a crisis after I became a millionaire. It nearly killed me. What I learned from this experience, I now pass on to you in this book.

I'm not going to tell you money doesn't matter – that would just be patronising. I will show you that it isn't all about the money through the stories that I share with you in *The Prosperity Code*.

This book is probably not what you expected when you picked it up. (You'll see why shortly.)

This book is designed to flip on its head many things you think about money. And it should be a wake-up call.

Basically, what I'm trying to say is this is unlike any other book about money or wealth you have read.

This book is the antidote to all the other books out there, which tell you to save money or cut back, stop spending money on lattes and invest it … wherever.

I'm not going to show you how to budget. I'm not going to tell you to put money into dozens of jars. Or stare into the mirror every morning and tell yourself you're rich when your bank account is barren.

*"I AM A BILLIONAIRE,
I AM A BILLIONAIRE..."*

Also... I can't pay my next phone bill

This book is not going to tell you that giving away all of your money is the root of happiness, or keeping it all is the only way to go.

Seriously, you know it already. Who am I to tell you what to do?

No, this book is not going to tell you what to do with your money.

It's going to do something greater. It's going to *transform* how you feel and think about money.

In fact, it's going to change how you feel about lots of different aspects of your life. (Money just tends to be, supposedly, the BIGGEST issue for many people.)

The Prosperity Code shows you a fun, easy, and simple way to think about money and attract money into your life. This book will also show you how to live a happier, more fulfilling life. I can teach you from my own experience and wisdom of some of the world's biggest wealth gurus.

Why it's NOT about the money

Debt, lousy credit, poverty, struggling to make ends meet … if only we had a bit more money we'd fix all these problems, right?

Wrong.

All the problems we see around money are not the real problem. They're the symptoms of a much bigger problem. And that problem is what we think, how we feel, and what we believe about life, love, and who we are.

Money does not change who we are. Money does not change how we feel. We give money that power. Because we give money that power, we can take it back again.

For some people, money is a tool that offers an opportunity to do great things – go travelling, pay for wonderful experiences, or do the things they love.

For some, money is the root of all evil. They believe people who are rich or have a lot of money are greedy and have exploited others to make their wealth. This is a very persuasive point amongst some theories.

Some people say money is nothing (yeah, right!). They carry on with their lives, seemingly without a care about financial issues. Or they at least *tell* everyone they don't care about money. (You may know a friend just like this, who is always going on about wealth not being important, but is constantly broke and asking for money.)

For others, money is everything. They cannot talk about or think about anything in their lives without coming back to money. They think about money all the time, they talk about money all the time, and everything they do is seen through the prism of money. Of course, this is fine if you have money, but if you don't, it becomes a burden.

For some people, money brings anxiety, fear, and worry. If you're stuck thinking about money all the time, it sucks the joy out of everything you do.

Be honest ... which one are you? What is closer to your way of thinking, right now?

Money has such a different effect from one person to the next. Give £1 million to two people, and you can be sure they'll handle it differently.

It all comes back to our beliefs and the way we see the world. Until you change your money beliefs, you will continue to have the same patterns and feelings around money that put you in the situation you're in now. That's true whether you are rolling in wealth or don't have two pennies to rub together.

Seriously, how many times have you read about lottery winners blowing their millions only to find themselves broke again in no time?

Some people give money too much power. This book is about how to get it back.

In the next 200 pages, I want to take you on a journey. This journey will introduce you to a process of transformation I've used in my own life and will help you break open your beliefs, tap into your intuition, and effortlessly attract abundance.

Sounds quite the promise, doesn't it? Well, keep reading, and you'll see.

How to use this book

The Prosperity Code is unlike any other book you've read on money, finance and wealth before. And it's organised in a pretty fun way, too.

Firstly, this book is structured around my personal story. Now, you may not have expected this to be a storybook, but there's a good reason I've written the book this way.

Long before writing, people told stories. Storytelling was how one generation passed down knowledge to another. Elders told their children stories, and they passed them onto their children. All human memories of experiences are through stories.

Using stories also helps us understand an idea or concept better than raw facts and figures. Some people gain more from reading a story and learning lessons easier this way.

I don't know whether I've lived a particularly strange or exciting life compared with some people ... but there are so many lessons in how I went from living in the USSR to building great wealth and finding happiness in London. (I hope you enjoy it!)

So that's my story.

As I wrote before, most money books push schemes, investments, and strategies onto you. They talk about how to save, how to budget, and how to cut back. Few talk about money beliefs.

I find it strange. Surely, nothing much else matters when it comes to money?

Unless we change the deeply held beliefs that drive our behaviour, we'll never change. Changing our beliefs is the road to a great relationship with money and wealth. It is the first step on the path to a happier, more joyful, and fulfilling life.

To help the lessons 'stick', there are exercises in each section.

See, you're not getting away with just sitting back and reading. I'm going to ask you to work on yourself as we go.

I recommend that you complete each exercise before moving onto the next. It's that simple.

Want results? Follow the structure. *The Prosperity Code* takes you on a journey of discovery about your own beliefs. To do that, you need to unpack it in the right order. I've structured the exercises in this way to get to the result you want quicker and more efficiently.

These are the same exercises I walk through with everyone who attends my workshops and meditation evenings. I know they work, and so I would implore you to trust in the process and dive in.

In other words ... just do it (I mean exercises)!

Even if you've done some training, seminars, esoteric practices, or personal development before and think you've done similar exercises, please don't skip them. (Yes, even YOU!)

If you have not done any financial or "spiritual" training before, well, you are in for a treat, and you're going to get the best of the best methods right now. That means you already have a psychology of abundance to find something that can help you and a technique that works (which took me years to discover and develop!).

So well done to you for finding this book! ☺

I would suggest using a separate notebook or journal to keep all your answers to the exercises in one place. It will be easier to refer to previous answers and track your journey. I have created that place on my website for you to help with your progress – visit www.prosperitycode.co.uk.

The next thing I would like you to do is to commit yourself.

You deserve all the success and happiness you want. From now on, I would like you to make a decision only to do things that make you happy, you love doing, or something that you are passionate about. Commit to love and respect yourself, and you will never need to sacrifice anything because of money. If, for you, this sounds impossible, read on, and I will show you how it is not just easy to do, but it is effortless.

I will show you in *The Prosperity Code*, why there is no need for 'sacrifice' in order to enjoy abundance all around you. Follow the exercises in this book, and you will unlock an approach that allows you to leave behind beliefs, blocks, and bad habits that repel money and do the things you love.

This book will help you live the life you want.

One more thing ... keeping an open mind

I'm going to be completely transparent with you.

("Oh no, what *is* she going to say ...?")

There is one idea we're going to come back to again and again in this book.

It is The Creator, or Energy of Creation or Unconditional Love.

Unconditional Love is the source of everything from which you can get direct knowledge and abundance. That's right! You can ask questions, you can ask for inspiration for ideas, and you can ask for help. If you're wondering whether you have the ability to do this right now, let me tell you, you do!

To demonstrate, let me ask you if this sounds familiar.

One day you walk out of your house and, suddenly, a thought comes into your mind: "I should go right today, and not left – not my usual route." And then you think, "Oh, what nonsense, I'm going to go my usual way." Then you go left, and you find yourself in a massive traffic jam, or there has been an accident, or you fall over and hurt yourself.

Something has happened which has negatively impacted you, and you think to yourself, "Oh, why didn't I listen to myself earlier?"

Do you ever have this kind of situation where you ask yourself, "Why didn't I listen to my inner voice?"

Well, that inner voice is your intuition. And I have good news and great news: The good news is everybody already has powerful intuition. The great news is if you're not listening to it enough, you can start right now!

Later in this book, I show you how to listen to your inner voice better, and I will share with you the method I discovered: Instant Transformation Technique (ITT). ITT is a method of fast improvements using a form of meditation or imagination to remove beliefs and change how you feel.

Oh, and this isn't one of those books where I tell you what you need to do, but then don't show you how to do it. I share with you everything in this book. I show you exactly how to use ITT even if you've never done anything like it before.

Have you done meditation before?

If this question makes you cringe, you have probably tried the wrong approach for you.

Here's a little list of everything I've personally tried. I attempted:

- Vipassana
- Transcendental meditation
- Chanting
- Dynamic meditation
- Yoga
- Contemplation
- Visualisation
- Shamanism
- Reiki
- Theta healing
- Buddhism
- Zen
- Reconnective healing
- Access bars and access consciousness
- Plus many, many more.

In some meditations I could never understand what was supposed to happen and what I was supposed to be doing. I hadn't the patience to sit and do nothing and think about nothing. And, besides, our brain is designed to think, as well as perform other tasks.

Talking about it, I could even write a book, *How To NOT Meditate And What Meditation Is Not!*

When I learned the Theta healing method, thanks to Vianna Stybal I finally realised what the true destination was, what was supposed to happen, and how you knew when it had worked.

Through this method, you learn how to achieve certain brain frequencies so you can live in a state that helps you achieve a stress-free, calmer, and more joyous state of mind.

It's important for me to show you from the beginning where we're heading in *The Prosperity Code*. If you don't feel this is for you, no problem at all – we're all different. But if you want to stay with the journey and discover more, then keep reading.

Stick with me, and I will show you exactly how to use the Instant Transformation Technique (ITT) to remove subconscious blocks, get rid of fears and problems, and live without stress or disease. And maybe a bit more besides …

Ready? Let's go…

My story

How not to be rich

By now, you've probably noticed my approach is a bit different from other authors. Most authors insist upon some kind of boastful introduction with pictures of themselves accepting awards or rubbing shoulders with celebs.

Just like this …

Sure, I've met some pretty amazing people ... but you don't *really* care about that, do you?

(Why did I include a picture of a giraffe above? Why not? It's just as relevant!)

If you're anything like me, you're probably sceptical right now. I would be.

Here's the thing: I'm not suggesting you do anything I haven't done. I used everything to show you in this book how to get where I am today. And where is that?

Well, I 'discovered' everything I share with you in these pages on my journey to becoming a millionaire by the time I was 29.

I built a multimillion-pound property portfolio, stocks and shares portfolio, and several successful businesses. I'm a partner in one of the UK's leading financial education and training businesses, www.wininvesting.com.

I also show you how not to be rich and how my beliefs about 'success' led me to the bottom of a deep depression. I got so sick that I couldn't even walk.

(Don't worry! Put that tissue away; there are no tears in this story. Fortunately, it has a happy ending.)

The reason I share my story isn't to impress you. It's to show you that anyone can do it.

I didn't inherit any wealth. I was born in Estonia, during the time of the USSR, and my family had very little money when I was growing up. I lived modestly (very, very modestly on just £5 a week to be exact!) when I first moved to London. But my lack of money never stopped me enjoying moments of great happiness and fun.

Having money is nothing if you cannot accept it into your life in an enjoyable way.

I'm telling you this to show you that I know what it takes to go to the top, get disillusioned and lost, hit rock bottom and go back to the top again and, ultimately, be happy. Read my story and decide for yourself whether my experiences are relevant and helpful to you.

By sharing my journey, I hope to show you that, no matter your situation right now, there is a fun, easy, and painless way to make money … and an enjoyable one. *The Prosperity Code* shows you how.

The accidental millionaire

There is a famous saying that goes:

"Whatever the mind can conceive and believe, the mind can achieve."

It's supposed to make a point that everything you have was previously only a thought. But I would disagree with that because I achieved far more than I could have ever imagined.

When children at my school were asked what they wanted to do when they grew up, I never could answer. I didn't want to be an engineer, or a doctor, or a teacher. So I kind of envied other children, because they knew what they wanted in their lives.

Me? I didn't know what I wanted to do. I never planned or wanted to be a millionaire. In fact, the concept of a millionaire didn't even exist in the USSR, where I grew up.

Then, Perestroika started, and my world changed.

I was finishing school and saw an advert for strawberry pickers in the UK. Now, this was sold to us as a "'lucrative'" opportunity, but I thought it looked good, and it would give me a chance to learn English as well.

To pursue this 'opportunity', I needed money for a flight. Back then, it was going to cost at least £500 for a return. (EasyjetEasyJet and the era of cheap flights didn't exist yet!)

"OK," I thought, "£500 it is!"

Now, £500 may not sound too much these days, but back then in Estonia, it was the equivalent of an annual wage. So without much thought, I left my last year of school and went to work in a liquor store. After that, I tried selling cheese at the market and various other goods to make enough money for a ticket to London.

Looking back, I was surprised to realise I already had the mindset of a winner.

I didn't dwell on hardships or the high price of an air ticket. I simply did what I had to do to get what I wanted. To me, there was no such thing as 'expensive'. Even then, I never restricted myself in my desires. If I knew I wanted it, I got it.

And it's no surprise it's served me well.

Why it's time to stop making excuses (and make your own luck)

If you looked at me as a child back in Estonia, nothing would point to the future that was ahead of me.

I came from a relatively normal Soviet Union family background. My father was an engineer, and my mother was a tailor. My parents certainly didn't have a millionaire mindset to pass on to me, yet we had a happy family.

Before, I told you that my school friends knew what they wanted to do to pursue their careers. I didn't know. So whenever I was asked at school what I wanted to do in life, my answer was, "A witch." It always made the class laugh. My second answer was that I wanted to be a secret service agent. (I even applied for an MI6 advert I saw on the Tube later. Sadly, they never called me back!)

Even though at that early age I didn't know what I wanted to be, I was certain of one thing: I knew I wanted something more. As I got older, I realised I was destined for something greater, which led me to follow the path to strawberry picking 'riches'.

Whenever I run a workshop, right at the start, I have a funny little quiz I have my students join in.

It's designed to challenge their preconceived ideas about their own success. And explains a lot about how I managed to become so successful at what I did and make the money I made.

So I start off like this and ask three questions:

Tatjana: How many of you speak English here?

(Normally everyone responds with "Yes")

Tatjana: How many of you have at least £50 in your bank account?

(Again the majority will say "Yes")

Tatjana: And, how many of you have at least a school education?

(Again everyone usually responds "Yes")

"Well," I say. "You are *way* ahead of me when I first came to London to pick strawberries."

How to start your life in London on £50

"So you're telling me I can't walk to Victoria station from here?"

The immigration officer stared at me in disbelief.

"Erm, not exactly," he said. "It's 20 miles away …"

Little did I know when I landed in Heathrow that getting about wasn't going to be *quite* as easy as I first thought.

It wouldn't have been too much of a problem, apart from the one little problem … I only had £50 in my pocket. That was it.

Why only £50?

Because I thought, why do I need money in London? Surely it's where all the money in the world is? Hmm.

I didn't speak very good English. I was educated to school

level, of course, which meant I could speak English, but if someone asked me something in real English, I couldn't understand. I could ask, "How do I get to Victoria?" but when they replied, I had no idea what they had said to me!

So there I was with £50 and hardly able to understand English, standing in front of an immigration officer trying to work out how I was going to get from Heathrow to London Victoria so I could catch a coach to the Norwich strawberry picking camp.

I'd come all this way. There was no way 20 miles was going to stop me. Okay, I'll find a way – and I did.

Back then – around 25 years ago – people used to hand out their travel cards once they had finished with them. I was rewarded with one without it costing a penny, and with my dreams of making it big in strawberry picking, I found a way to get to Victoria and onward to what I believed was going to be lucrative work.

Staying with strangers

Well, picking strawberries wasn't quite the lucrative opportunity I'd been led to believe. "Seriously? What a shock!" you're probably thinking. But it wasn't bad either. I was used to garden work and picking berries, so it wasn't too hard and the money was quite good.

When it came to paying for my school of English, I decided it would be better to be in London as I had a friend there I could stay with.

I arrived back in the capital with my £50, of course (after I paid all that money for my education to a school of English), and it happened to be Christmas Eve. Now Christmas Eve in London is magical with all the Christmas decorations and lighting. Unfortunately, it's not so magical when you need to get anywhere. (You're spotting a recurring theme here, I guess!)

I was so mesmerised by the beauty of London that I missed the last train. I didn't know about night buses then, so I stopped a cab and asked him to take me to where my friend lived.

The taxi driver told me the fare would usually be about £25 but, because it was Christmas Day already, it was double fare.

"I'll take you," he said. "But you need to show me you have £50 first." Of course, there went my last £50.

Again, there was a catch: I didn't know the exact address of my friend. I just knew generally where he lived. Did that stop me? Of course not!

The taxi driver drove me to the station near where my friend lived, and I thought I could find my way to his house from there. As you can imagine, it didn't work out like that. It looked completely different and was unrecognisable at night. It was 2 a.m., and everything looked new. I couldn't find my way. I was lost, and I was cold, and I was hungry. I wanted to sleep, and I had no money.

So what did I do in this situation?

I knocked on the first door I came to that had lights on, and this guy opened the door. Right away, I said to him, "Hello, I'm Tania from Estonia. I have no money. I'm hungry, and I want to sleep."

The guy looked at me a little funny and then thoughtfully replied, "Okay, come in," and gave me a place to sleep for the night.

In the morning, he fed me breakfast and walked with me to help me find my friend. I traced my steps to where I thought my friend was living, and I knocked on the door.

Again, a long-haired guy answered the door, and I announced to him, "Hello, I'm Tania from Estonia. I'm looking for my friend, Dmitri."

I was about to get a shock. "Oh, Dmitri left for the Christmas holidays for two weeks. He's not going to be back for a while," was the answer.

I couldn't believe it! "What do you mean he left for two weeks?" I said. "I have no money and no food."

This man told me not to worry and invited me in to wait until Dmitri returned by sleeping on the kitchen sofa.

What an introduction to life in London! As you can imagine, I now believe that London is the friendliest and nicest city in the world!

It didn't stop there, either. The first person who opened the door on Christmas Day happened to become my first husband. We got married on the 1st of May ... but that's a whole other story.

(What, Tatjana?! You can't leave that story there, seriously! Well, I'm going to. That's for another book. :))

Setting up in business

In the first month of life in London, I learned to live on £5 a week, riding on the subway without paying the fare, and buying food past its expiry date for a penny.

You can only do that for so long before you know you need to make a change. That's when I decided to go and work as a salesperson on a commission-only basis to bring in some big money.

The job involved calling up businesses in the former USSR and inviting them to London for training. When these people came to London, we treated them like VIPs. We'd meet them and take care of them by driving them to restaurants or taking them shopping.

It was hard work initially, and it took me three months to close the first deal and get some money. But it turned out it was good money.

Really good money.

That's when I thought, "Why not set up my *own* business; I could do it better?"

My friend and I set up our own sales business, selling educational programmes for companies in the former Soviet Union. Because the free market and free economy was a new concept, these companies had to adjust to the new landscape. They needed help understanding how the free market economy worked. Education could help them.

Our seminars would cover everything from marketing to promoting business and accountancy. We even hired professors from the London School of Economics to deliver the lectures for us.

When it came to selling the events, our strategy was pretty simple. We would call any company in the former USSR we thought had money – in oil, gas, telecoms, or metallurgy – and invite them to seminars in London. To make things more interesting, we also included cultural and entertainment activities.

It worked well. *Really* well. We started to hire more and more girls to help make calls. And, sometimes, even when it didn't work well, we still managed to stumble upon some amazing and weird opportunities.

Why diamonds are for the poor ...

We were running our business now from our house, working towards finding new contracts and getting clients to come to our seminars in London.

We had multiple phone lines and a few people making international calls. On one wonderful day, we received a British Telecom bill of over £8000.

We checked our bank account and realised we only had £4000 there – so we were £4000 short.

What would you do in this situation?

Of course, withdraw all the cash and go shopping for diamonds! So that's exactly what we did. Brilliant! I split what was left of the money in our bank account with my partner, so we had £2000 each, and we went jewellery shopping.

Why jewellery? Because it is a good investment, we thought! And if it is an investment, it is not a reckless use of money.

As a result, I got a diamond and sapphire ring (which I still have to this day), this is it below and my friend also bought something nice.

We came home, had tea while admiring our purchases, and made plans for the future.

You see, it is very logical what happens when you have no money whatsoever.

So, what do you think happens next?

We concluded that as we were just 22, full of enthusiasm, and running a business in London, money should come soon. However, money did not arrive the next day or the day after, and we had no money for food either.

A few days later, my mother came to visit from Estonia and bought us some food. That was amazing! A couple of weeks later, one of the girls landed a deal, and a nice sum of money hit our account. We knew money would come from somewhere – there were no other options!

Riding the train to opportunity

"Oh, girl … you really don't understand what we do, do you?"

It wasn't the best start to a conversation, I admit. But it was about to get crazy.

One of the girls I hired had just explained to one company exec the programme we were offering to metallurgical plants. The only problem was that it turned out that it wasn't a metal plant. It was a transport company – a railway.

While most people would have quietly apologised, hung up, and moved on. Not us.

As the conversation continued, the person at the other end of the phone revealed what they were really looking for.

"We're railways, not metal," the exec told her. "What we're looking for is to privatise railways in Russia ... if you have anything relevant to this, we might be interested."

Well, you'd never guess what? We could.

Of course, I told him we could offer them many things ... as long as they paid us lots of money.

We did, and we told the exec we could deliver a presentation on the privatisation of railways.

It turns out the guy on the phone was very influential. He gathered a group of 30 or 40 directors of all the regional railways and ministry of Russian railways.

"OK," he told us. "We have a group. Send us the invoice."

Basically, we didn't hold our breaths. We really didn't expect them to pay ... and then, we got the payment, and we were like, OOPS!

That's how we started. We got the best, most expensive accountants in the City on our side and the best law firm we could (not) afford. When we called our lawyers, it turned out they were the firm who helped privatise British Rail.

This law firm had been through the whole privatisation process. They agreed they would do the presentation for our delegation because it was very high profile, and these rail firms would be highly desirable clients for the law firm. And the best news was they would do it for free.

That's what happened. The law firm organised a whole week of lectures, presentations, and visits to various railways for our delegation. It was like an experience exchange. The clients were delighted with what they received (and we were delighted banking that invoice).

How I didn't become an alcohol business tycoon

Any time I saw an opportunity, I would follow it. Sometimes it worked, and sometimes it failed. Often, quite spectacularly.

One time, I just decided to become an alcohol business tycoon.

We started inviting Russian and Ukrainian companies across to the UK for food and drink exhibitions.

We made a deal with a Kiev sparkling wine plant. Kiev sparkling wines were of top quality, so we knew it would be possible to grow sales quickly.

We sent the wines to a laboratory for analysis, hired a marketing person to promote the brand, and won a contract with Europa Foods, who was happy to take half a lorry of our champagnes for their shops.

Our suppliers basically gave us the lorry full of alcohol for free, and we only needed to pay them after we sold it. It seemed like a great deal.

The wine producers came to London and met my partner and me in person (which probably cost them more than the lorry of champagne itself).

Money-wise, I really believed we were onto a winner ... until the lorry turned up at the English border.

What I hadn't factored in was the fact that alcohol had a 500% import tax. Of course, I didn't have the £25,000 I needed to pay the tax at that stage, so my attempt to become an alcohol tycoon ended *very* quickly.

Flying high with another opportunity

But I didn't give up. I saw opportunities everywhere. Where other people wouldn't necessarily see them or wouldn't necessarily do something about it, I took action.

I built the business and explored ways to make money every way I could. I saw what needed to be done ... and did it.

We got involved in the aerospace and aircraft building industry after calling contacts in Russia and discovering they were all coming to the UK for the Farnborough Air Show. These were huge aircraft production and helicopter manufacturing plants. Straight away, we saw another business opportunity. They told us they had half a million dollars budgeted for these kinds of shows, so it was obviously something we had to follow!

For five years in a row, we called aerospace and weapons industry businesses six months before the airshow. We offered to look after them, organise transport and interpreters for exhibitions.

We hired more girls into the business and kept following up opportunities, wherever we saw them. We called relatives in Russian and asked for their copies of the Yellow Pages to be posted to us so we could find anything relevant (back then, not many companies were on the internet).

There was also a moment when we almost became involved in fashion manufacturing and wholesale ... but that didn't end *quite* so well.

How failed fashion drove me to more diamonds

Our next venture took us into the world of fashion. Well, *almost*.

The then-boyfriend of my partner gave us a tip-off. He said that there was a booming business in Israel selling clothes, and it was an area that was really taking off. He was Jewish himself and had a shop in Aldgate East where a lot of wholesalers were based, and he told us a lot of the buyers were from Israel.

Of course, we decided this was going to be our next big business opportunity. As I was the only one of us that could speak English and had the documents to travel, I was packed off to Hungary where we were told they manufactured clothes cheaply.

Without knowing *anything* about the fashion retail business and without knowing *anything* about fashion wholesale or manufacturing, I found myself flying to Hungary to find out where to buy cheap clothes. I didn't know where to start, so I began at a local market where they sold garments. I asked the stall owners who were the producers of the clothes they were selling, and they gave me the name of a factory.

Off I went to the factory and spoke to the owner and placed an order with them for 10,000 tops. I had to wait a week until the order was ready, and then I had the order shipped to Israel. I flew to Israel and paid the import tax and embarked on a tour of wholesalers and dealers trying to sell my cargo of clothes. Very quickly, I found someone who would buy the units. After long and heavy negotiations, we agreed on a price and organised a date and time for delivery. All the signs were – this was going to be the deal to make us rich. It was a sure thing … or so I thought.

The night before I was to deliver the order to the wholesalers, I stayed in a hotel with all the bags of clothing ready to take to the dealer in the morning. I called a taxi to collect me in the morning and loaded all these huge bags of clothes into his car. Before I had a chance to jump into the taxi myself, he drove off.

As he was driving away, desperation hit, and the realisation that I had no more stock and no money left. Everything was gone!

You can imagine just how distraught I was at that moment. I called my friend and told her everything and that I'd been robbed (although I wasn't 100% sure she believed me). I went to the airport to return home and realised I had no money on me. However, I did have a business credit card available with a limit of £20,000, so I wasn't *completely* out of money.

And that was the second time I bought diamonds for myself! I bought some beautiful white gold and diamond earrings and a ring set to keep my spirits up! Here they are…

Hey, I deserved it, OK?!

I believe that whatever happens, I'll always manage to pay off a credit card – even if it was like £50 a week – but at least I had some diamonds. People say diamonds are only for the rich, but in reality, anyone can afford them. Forget the advice that you shouldn't spend money when you are broke; you should always keep yourself happy. If you are sad or stressed, go and treat yourself. You deserve it. And have faith the universe will take care of you.

Everything I wanted, I manifested

When I became a millionaire at 29, it wasn't by accident. I was wholly responsible for the wealth I created through investment deals and the business. I created my own financial wealth.

It is fair to say that everything I have ever wanted, I have succeeded in obtaining. To me, that is one of the strongest beliefs that drive my life. Nothing is more powerful than knowing you can create wealth and value from simply believing you can. It all hinges on three points: faith, passion, and taking action, all of that with love.

Taking action on your needs and desires is essential to living fulfilling life.

If there's anything to take from this book, it is to start taking action on things you love and are passionate about to move towards where you really want to be, rather than letting life slip by. If you don't have your own dreams, you end up being at the mercy of someone else's plan.

A positive mindset and true goals are paramount. I always knew that I could achieve anything. If something did not work, find out why and change your approach.

Making so much money when you don't know how to be happy or enjoy wealth has a dark side, though.

I suffered a crisis because I thought I had achieved it all. I believed: that was it, and there was nothing else for me to do or look forward to. In this case, I succumbed to a belief about what society perceives to be right. Being misled affected me psychologically and physically in a very dark way.

These collective consciousness beliefs focus on what you should do or achieve in life. They are very powerful and extremely persuasive and can lead to serious problems if you buy into them. And that's exactly what happened to me.

How becoming a millionaire almost killed me

"Leave me alone ... I don't want to live!"

It's hard to believe that after reading everything I've just written that I was the one screaming those words.

Everything I wanted, I achieved, and much more. Yet, I never planned out what I would be doing as far ahead as ten years. Take a guess when my crisis hit.

If you've ever attended Tony Robbins' seminars, you may know he has a process called the Rapid Planning Method. Using this method, you set outcomes for one week, 30 days, one year, five years, ten years, and all the way up to twenty years.

Of course, anyone can make plans for up to a year. I honestly felt that if I could achieve so much in one year, I could achieve anything. So, what's the point of putting down on paper what I want to achieve in ten or twenty years?

BIG mistake.

I didn't know it then, but I had issues with the future. I couldn't imagine it. I thought I would run out of things to do if I kept going this fast. I thought I had an abundant mindset, but that came crashing down and nearly killed me.

Let's recap where I was to this point: I had a happy childhood, then I moved country. I created a business from nothing, made my money, and had a family, two children, and bought a few houses. That's a good life plan for most people.

I had the money. I travelled the world and visited many, many amazing places. But I didn't find it very appealing or exciting because I had no purpose. I didn't know how to enjoy myself and how to have fun. Even though I had a family and money and had all these experiences, I pretty much thought my life was lived well, and the plan was fulfilled.

It felt like I didn't have any purpose in life anymore, and I fell into a deep depression. After ten years, I thought that there was nothing else that this world had to offer. I was holding a delusional belief that I'd done it all and seen it all.

In reality, I'd only seen hard work and learned how to run a business and make money. I didn't even master that because I never had the goal of building a billion-pound multinational corporation. It didn't interest me.

But having had all these experiences and having achieved so much, I thought it was done and over. I was stepping into what we would call a 'self-destruction' programme in my mid-thirties.

When a person doesn't want to live anymore, consciously or subconsciously, they step onto a path of self-destruction, both mentally and physically.

It got to the stage where I was in unbearable pain. I would attempt to go into my garden. The children would be playing, sun shining and birds singing. Yet, for me, it was a living hell because I was in so much pain, which I created.

That was rock bottom for me. It was so unbearable I felt I had to die. But my partner wouldn't let me – he really cared for me. He would carry me around and take me outside, and I would be screaming at him, "Leave me alone. I don't want to live."

Basically, he wouldn't allow me to die. He did the right thing, although it must have been tough to deal with me at that time.

It was almost impossible to live with intense pain like that, so I had to find a cure and get well again, even though doctors told me it was impossible and I was incurable.

And then, one day, it was over. I passed that stage, and that's when I realised, "Okay, I'm not dying anymore, and I don't want the pain, so I have to recover."

Now, I had a purpose in life: to find a way to recover.

When I got through that period, I realised there was only one way to go – up. I started asking myself, "Where do I go from here? If I want to get well, then I need to do something," and so I began searching for ways to get better.

I saw doctors, and they told me I was incurable, so I began my own research, which started me on a journey of self-discovery.

Self-discovery, strong Chi and serendipity

Once you make a firm decision, it feels like the whole universe is on your side. Everyone starts helping you. Everything falls into place.

Sometimes things just appear at the right time in your life.

These days, everyone is all over social media all the time. At that stage, however, I was seldom on social media. I don't know what encouraged me to open my laptop and check Facebook that day, but when I did, I saw an advert on my newsfeed that was almost perfectly tailored to me and my situation.

The advert was for a seminar with a picture of the same woman at 30 and 55. In the image of her at 30, she looked like her life was over. It turned out she had been paralysed from the neck down from an accident.

But in the image of her at 55, she looked like she was 18 – it was incredible. It was definitely her, but she was transformed. I thought, "Okay, I definitely need to see this lady."

So that's where it started.

I went to this seminar to see her. I met the organiser, who told me the Facebook advert I saw was only online for a minute until the admins of the group removed it. I managed to see it in that tiny gap of time – like it was posted just for me!

From this seminar, the lady recommended a man called David Verdesi, who dedicated his whole life to searching for power and immortality and met all the saints and most amazing people of our modern times, including Mother Teresa. David was the next person I went to see. Then I was off to visit shamans in Peru for three months, and then I went to Bali to work with some amazing healers there.

One lady had such strong Chi in her hands she could literally electrocute you. One day, she electrocuted me on my forehead so strongly, I jumped maybe a metre in the air on a massage table! I also met a Chinese healer from Shaolin who had a similar power, but stronger, and could electrocute you with his energy and perform healing.

Through meeting all these people, my process of self-discovery began. I witnessed many miracles and met a lot of people with superpowers.

When an uneventful moment turns out to be a big realisation

When I was still in search of a cure for my health issues, one of my teachers offered a chance to travel to Peru to meet shamans and try ancient medicine, so I did.

I organised a tour with the local guide, boarded a plane to Lima, then Pucallpa, then a boat to a village in the Peruvian Selva. In that village, every household had a shaman. I met Elisa and her teacher (Maestra), who helped me on my path to recovery.

I spent a lot of time there in ceremonies at night and doing not much else during the day.

One day I was given a book to read by Osho. At that period in life, I was not very much interested in reading that type of literature, so I randomly opened a book on page 69 and read about enlightened people of the new age. It said that in our times we could have the 'New Enlightened', who can be rich and enjoy their life experience to the full and share their knowledge and wisdom with others without pain or sacrifice.

Straight away I labelled Osho as pop culture of the spiritual and esoteric world. Little did I know that was really the most sensible thing I have ever read in my life.

I had a vague understanding of what enlightenment actually was from what I heard or read. It was more like an image of sacrifice, suffering, sainthood, solitude, or austerity. It also had nothing to do with the real-life or modern world we lived in. Or so I thought then.

Looking for the Magic Pill

"What a load of NONSENSE!"

That was my response to 99% of answers I tried to the problems I was having, back when I suffered my collapse.

You know that feeling when you've been told something for like the 300th time, and you just start to lose patience because you know it's BS?

Yes, well, that's where I was. I'd just been told by another healer those immortal words, "The answer is within you," and I wasn't buying it.

Sure, it may be true, but when you're desperately searching for answers, you don't want to hear it. Obviously, I didn't understand it back then as I do now ... but at the time, it was really irritating.

You see, as fantastic as all these experiences were, my problem wasn't getting solved quickly enough for me. I wanted to feel better and be back to my wonderful self. It still seemed like I was a long way from that point.

I had money, so I was basically after a Magic Pill. Like most people, I didn't actually want to do anything; I just wanted to pay my money and get the problem fixed once and for all.

After travelling the globe on this year of self-discovery and doing meditations of all sorts, somebody recommended a healer to me. By this stage, I was happy to try anything. Her name was Natalia, and I booked a session with her. For the first time, I did a session, and I experienced instant healing – what a miracle!

Now, I know what you're thinking … really, Tatjana? Instant? Yes, it was!

When I say 'instant healing', I mean it in the literal sense. There was a flash of light, and I was well again. It sounds crazy when you see it written down like this or you hear someone telling you about it, I understand.

But, for me, it worked. I was healed. But only for two weeks, though. After two weeks, my pain returned (because it turned out that being ill was serving me greatly!) The experience convinced me, however, that it was possible to get well and to change in an instant.

From that moment on, I wanted to learn what she did and what this form of healing was. This was my introduction to a new instant healing method.

How I learnt to out-eat bodybuilders in Bali

"You're finished with that, right?"

I was staring at the plates of unfinished food sat in front of two huge bodybuilders on the table next to me.

Equally, they were staring back at me in awe at first having finished the huge meal I'd eaten and how I now had ambitions on what was left of their food.

I was in Bali, and I was making a name for myself with my incredible appetite in the town where I was staying. I had good reason.

My recovery was all about finding my taste for life again, which meant finding more joyful and pleasurable experiences. One of the most pleasurable activity for me was eating as I needed to put back on all the weight I'd lost. With my height of 180cm, I was down to just 50kg (which was my weight when I was 13 years old)!

In Bali, I was famous in a place called Cafe Cafe. (It was a cafe called Cafe. Weird, I know!)

I would go there every day, and when I ordered a dessert, say tiramisu, the waitress already knew me, and she would ask, "How many?"

My record was five.

There was another cafe where they had fresh ducks from the rice fields running around. They would catch them and cook them without even marinating them. They were completely fresh, and it tasted like the greatest delicacy in the world.

I used to go to the gym with all these bodybuilders – really big guys – and after we would go to this cafe and order lunch.

These huge guys would order one or two chickens or a chicken and a duck. I would order three ducks, two chickens, one salad, a coconut, and one dessert. Every time.

They would look at me and say, "Tatjana, what are you eating? It looks so tasty!"

Then they would order another chicken and wouldn't be able to finish it. Which was great news for me. "No worries, I'll finish it for you!"

That was how I started my physical recovery in Bali. I went from 50kg and to 60kg when I came home. I put on 10 kilos in three months. And I had an amazing time doing it!

How to transform lives (no matter what the situation)

Once I had discovered the power of Instant Transformation, there was no holding me back. I used this powerful technique to change my beliefs and my life.

When people saw the transformation in me, they were curious. They wanted to find out what this miracle cure was that worked so well. That's when I became a healer, working with people on whatever they wanted to change.

After all these years, I've risen to become one of the instructors and healers that can really help people to make the shift. Now, when I work with people privately on their issues, I charge £1000 an hour. This method can help people with any issues or questions they have, no matter how strange.

I have clients come to me and ask, "Tania, I have a court case tomorrow – can you fix it?"

At this point, I usually say to them, "Er, it's tomorrow … did you think about it earlier?!"

Even if it's something as urgent and immediate as this, we work on their beliefs and find a way to resolve it. We see why the person created the court case and why they needed it in their life. Then we make it go away or make it work in their favour. You see, every situation can offer an opportunity.

If you've created a situation or problem, it's for a reason. You want to gain or avoid something. We just uncover what it is and what you really want and use the situation to your advantage.

Someone may come to me and say, "I've got a job interview – can you check if I'm going to get it?"

If I see they don't get the job because, say, the interviewer says something that my client doesn't like and cannot accept. The client could snap, show outrage, and ruin the interview. The reason they don't get the job in that situation is usually because of a lack of some resources (virtues). So I explain that if they change their beliefs and replace these beliefs with virtues, they will get it.

"Would you like to do it?" I say. They agree, and then we work towards the result. I tell them what needs to change, for example, we download patience, acceptance, humility, and respect, and after certain changes, the interview looks more successful and calm. We work until I see that situation is fully resolved, and the client gets the job.

I even had cancer patients coming to me because doctors told them the same they told me once, that they could not help them, and either it was too late, hopeless, or incurable. After working with me, these people are alive and well after a few years so far. I even worked with an HIV positive client to improve their situation.

I had a lady at my *Money Magic* seminar who invested all the money she had into an off-plan property and then the developer had to freeze the project for a few years. She had almost given up on that project, but after we worked on the issue at the seminar and removed the block for her sabotaging her abundance, the next day, still at the seminar, she got a message from a developer, saying she could view her property next week. That was a miracle to her!

> "I just finished *Money Magic* course with Tatjana Valujeva and received direct results, literally 15 minutes ago. I got a text message from my developer (it was a long-overdue completion of the project delayed by 3 years), that I was invited to view my apartment…"

Alena G

You can see her testimonial on my web site https://prosperitycode.co.uk

This method also works really well with people who feel unfulfilled or depressed despite being wealthy and having a good life. Figuring out why someone is unhappy, even though they have everything, is one of my favourite types of session because I personally went through that.

I had people solving ongoing issues from working on their blocks at a seminar in a day. I witnessed many miracles and instant healings and have many testimonials, which you can watch on my site www.prosperitycode.co.uk .

I learn so much from my students and clients, and it's one of the joys I get from being a teacher and a healer and having discovered Instant Transformations.

It allows me to be constantly surprised and delighted with the results we get and even from the gifts my students send me when they experience an incredible transformation. I love getting chocolates, flowers, jewellery and other things, of course, but the most amazing gift of all is a new success story or an instant healing for one more person like this:

> "I really enjoyed ... *Money Magic,* when I came here I was feeling very heavy, but ... this course it has changed my life ... I see how to use money, how to become financially free, how to live in abundance... it's really been an amazing experience... I will definitely recommend this course to people."
>
> Ali

Now, I work with a whole range of people, including celebrities, to change all aspects of their lives, from health and wealth to love and relationships.

I'll reveal more about the process and how Instant Transformations can transform your money and wealth beliefs later in the book. And I would love to hear your success story too – that would be the greatest gift!

When Santa made me cry (and showed me what's important)

A few years back, when I had just about recovered from my illness, I was cleaning the kids' room, and I found a Post-It note stuck to the window. It was crumpled and was already losing its colour, so I could tell it was a few years old. It had been completely forgotten behind the painting.

I pulled it off the window and looked at what was written on the note and saw it was addressed to Santa Claus. When I read the rest of the note, I started crying.

The note said, "Dear Santa Claus, I want my mommy to be able to run and play with us again." I recognised my daughter's handwriting.

When I saw that note, I couldn't believe how careless I was to let down my children so much. It felt like I was so selfish to be consumed with just my issues. At that moment, I made a promise to myself that I would always be healthy and happy for my own sake, so I could be a good example for my kids.

When a six-year-old girl's only wish to Santa Claus is for her mother to be healthy and be able to play with her, it is very touching. She didn't ask for any toys; she just wanted what truly mattered. I was amazed at my children's wisdom and empathy.

Children born in abundance don't care much for money; they don't care for toys. For them, these things hold no greater meaning. It's like okay, food is just food, money is just money.

This helped me realise just how much more spiritually advanced our generation of children is and how much they can teach us. There is a belief that abundance and lots of money can spoil people. Which is completely untrue, and my kids showed me that.

Children are more in touch with themselves. They haven't been retrained by adults yet about how they should live. Kids still have that natural state of joy and happiness, and beliefs don't cloud their judgement or their thinking.

It's really important to understand that your happiness is unconditional. Children can be happy, even in poverty. They find creative ways to entertain themselves.

Like many my age, I didn't have a computer in my childhood or the internet, so I would make myself various toys out of what we had, or we'd invent games. We would run around instead of sitting at home, and we would play games with friends and just be joyful.

It's just more proof that to be happy we don't really need a lot of money because all the joy, fun, playfulness and excitement are unconditional.

This was a critical lesson I learned when I had lots of money but still found myself unhappy.

Being happy is important. So, let's leave my story for now and first understand what it means to be fulfilled.

The secret to being happy

"I went to a bookstore and asked the saleswoman, 'Where's the self-help section?' She said if she told me, it would defeat the purpose"

GEORGE CARLIN

You and money

You thought this book was all about me giving you advice, didn't you?

Haha. Big mistake!

What this book is really about is YOU. Or, more accurately, what money and success means to you.

I said there were exercises for you to complete and now seems like the perfect time to kick off with one. There's nothing like getting deep in the first few pages of a book and exposing your vulnerabilities early on, is there?

Great, I knew you'd understand.

So let's get started and discover what comes to mind when you think about money.

Grab a pen and take a few minutes to complete this little exercise.

I want you to think about how money makes you *feel*. You're going to have to be in tune with your body on this. Through this process, we want to discover what happens in your body when you hear (or read) the word 'money'.

- What is money for you?
- What is your image of money or your association with money?
- What does it mean to you to have an unlimited amount of money?
- What does it mean to you to have no money?

To get started, write down: "Money for me is ..." and complete each sentence with your own thoughts or feelings. Make a list as long as possible. Try to get to 20 to 30, at least.

Be honest. Like REALLY honest. Don't hold back. Get everything down good, bad, or ugly, about how you feel about money.

And don't turn the page until you've done this exercise. IT IS IMPORTANT!

Go on, write it down right now on in the space below.

....

....

....

....

....

....

....

....

....

Have you done it yet? If not, don't even think about turning the page. If you have, go on.

So, what did you write?

Was there anything on your list of thoughts and feelings that surprised you? Was it mainly positive or mainly negative? Or did you hit a complete blank?

There is no right or wrong with this exercise. It is what it is.

Your answer is completely personal. How one person sees money is totally different from how another person sees money.

When I ask the students in my seminars and workshops to complete this exercise and list their thoughts, the list usually contains words like:

- Freedom
- Control
- Power
- Betrayal
- Happiness
- Lifestyle
- Competition
- Something to fight over
- Choice
- Time
- Hard work
- Security
- Evil
- Pain
- Worry
- Danger

Do you recognise any of these from your own list?

Although this is a short list, it does highlight the contradictory nature of beliefs about money. How can one person see money as freedom, and another see it as evil? How can we hold both thoughts in our mind at the same time? That's what we're going to find out.

Why this doesn't need to be hard

The last thing you need is to read *another* book about money.

Most personal wealth books give you the kind of advice that suggests with great certainty what to do with your money.

Scrimp here. Save here. Take 10% of your income and invest. Put your money into property. Put your money into stocks and shares, they tell you.

Look, if you need advice on what to do with your money, you can find advice for free, anywhere. The world is awash with advice about money. What to do with it, how to save it, how to spend it, and how to make it. But, seriously, for all the advice out there, what has it done?

This freely available advice makes little difference to how people act and behave when it comes to investing or spending money. We're at crisis point. People have never been more anxious, more uptight, and more hung up on money.

Look at the facts: in the UK, the average debt is £30,000 per person. That's high. Higher than the average wage. Yes, that's right. The average debt level is more than most people earn.

There's a spiritual cost to this. Financial concerns and debt anxiety affect how most adults live their lives. They literally walk around feeling the burden of debt and money worries every day, in everything they do. They live smaller lives, fearful and worried. Then, they pass that anxiety onto their children, and the cycle continues.

If we want to stop the cycle, no book about saving pennies or dividing your salary into jars is going to make a difference. Because the reason these issues get worse – even with all the free advice out there – is they don't address the real problem.

How to be happy

Money is not happiness. (Does that shock you when you read that?)

Money is just one part of our whole life. We're all beings who rely on balance in different parts of our lives.

Balance is what helps us to be happy. The balance between all the most important elements we have in life.

To get an idea of how balanced you are, rate yourself right now on the wheel of life below, and let's see how smooth your ride is.

Be honest. In which areas do you feel you're strong or put a lot of focus? Which areas need improvement or are weak in your life right now?

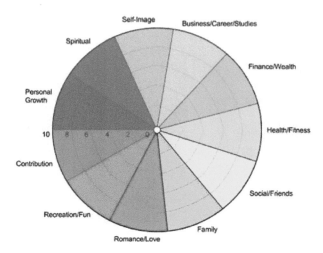

After you mark where you are in each category, connect the dots and see how round your wheel of life is.

Does it look like a perfect circle?

If you said yes, then you will have a smooth ride on that wheel of life. You may not be exactly where you want to be, but you're more likely to be happy.

If your 'wheel' is all over the place, you have abundance in some areas of your life and not others. What happens when you have a wonky wheel? You're in for a bumpy ride!

If you focus solely on money and wealth and ignore the spiritual or relationship side of your life, you're going to be unhappy.

Seriously, how many unhappy millionaires and billionaires do we see who just wish they'd spent more time with their children or been there for their parents?

Equally, if you focus too much on socialising and relationships and neglect your finances, you'll find yourself burdened with unpaid bills and worry.

What I've learned from my journey is that it's never about one thing. It's about everything. It's about finding the balance. The worst advice you can follow is to focus only on one thing.

The good news is: now you know. If your 'wheel' shows you doing well in career and wealth, but weak in relationships or spirituality, you know what you need to do.

A way to abundance

What's the definition of success? Achieving things? But what happens when you run out of things to accomplish?

Here's the problem with making wealth accumulation the measure of your success: it's a very narrow way of thinking that can cause a crisis – like mine.

How often do we hear about the millionaire who is depressed and doesn't know what to do with him or herself? How often do we hear about people who are serial overachievers who struggle to find meaning and joy in what they do? The challenge is always keeping a true meaning of life in sight.

You've heard my story now. I honestly thought I believed that creating financial abundance was the way to success ... until this episode in my life showed me how wrong I was. I had issues with my values. I couldn't imagine or believe I would run out of things to do. I was going fast ... and that's why it "ended" on the ten-year mark because everything I wanted I had ticked off the list in my subconscious.

Here's an exercise to test your abundance mindset.

Write down 100 things that you want. The 100 things can be anything – material things, experiences, basically anything that you want to get or want to achieve. Go on, do it now. I'll wait. Seriously, put the book down and don't come back until you're absolutely, positively sure you've written as many as you can.

Now, it tells you how abundant your mindset is based on how easily you hit 100 things on your list. What I discover from teaching my *Money Magic* workshops and Prosperity Code seminars is:

- If you're not used to this kind of challenge, you'll probably run out of things to write after about 10.
- If you've thought about exercises like this before or have done something similar, you may start struggling after 50 or 60.
- If you hit 100, congratulations!

(I've never had anyone manage to write down 100 before I explained this exercise further!)

So this is the first part of the exercise. The next part is going to blow your mind.

Take this list, and whenever you get or achieve one of the things on the list, you can cross it out, BUT you need to write down two new items on the list. Yes, ADD to the list.

This means you create a list of achievements you can *never* possibly complete.

When a list shrinks, it sends out a message that your life is shrinking too. When you add more achievements each time you tick one off, your life is growing in its wishes and desires.

This is such a great exercise to do – now, you'll probably want to go back and try having a go at getting all 100 items on the list.

Go on, do it – even if they're relatively minor or you think they're trivial, you'll be able to tick them off quickly and start expanding your list even more.

You feel better for ticking items off and creating your abundant future. There is no such thing as a small or big wish; it is still a wish.

Win–win!

Why overachieving is seriously overrated (and what to do instead)

How did you find that exercise? There's a good reason I wanted you to do it at this stage in the book.

It's vital to learn to love yourself and to love life. I never really understood before what it meant not to want to live until I had depression. I didn't even know I had depression.

I hit a plateau where I felt I'd seen it all and done it all in life. For most people, a life plan consists of a few points: have a family and kids, buy a house and the latest modern life goal: make a million. I had all that by 29, and I still was not happy, and I didn't know why.

So I did what rich people are meant to do: travel, party, spend. The problem was there was no purpose in any of it. I didn't know how to enjoy all the gifts of life, so I felt like life had nothing else to offer. But this was such a delusion; how wrong I was!

There is so much to see in this life and so much to explore and enjoy. That's why this practice is super amazing and greatly useful for each dream you achieve so you never run out of wishes and desires. As long as you want and wish, and as long as you have desires, and you enjoy them, you live. The stronger your passion for life is, the stronger your life force is.

The truth about money

"Children are much wiser than adults in many ways"

TATJANA VALUJEVA

What is money, anyway?

Money isn't everything. There, I said it.

You may find that a strange thing to say in a book about money. But then this isn't any old book.

Money really is not going to change how happy you are. That isn't saying it can't improve your lifestyle or add more comfort to your life. What I mean is: money cannot give you what you really desire.

Sure, money could amplify your existing state of mind or your mood, like alcohol or chocolate (or whatever other comfort things you use to help you relax or feel better).

But your happiness and joy are not dependent on money. Nor should they be. It means you cannot really use money as an excuse for not succeeding or being depressed. We've been programmed to believe money will solve all the issues in your life. The problem is, this belief is somewhat different from the reality.

Our understanding of what money is and what money means has become distorted. Before people had money, it never used to be this way.

A very brief history of money

Once upon a time, there was no money in the world. The concept didn't even exist. People hunted or picked food and made clothes. They had everything they needed. There was no need for money.

As populations grew at the advent of the agricultural revolution, people decided to barter for things and invented natural exchange, for example, a sack of potatoes for a chicken. This form of exchange became more sophisticated: gold, shells, tulip bulbs, metals, or stones.

As trade routes opened up and traders travelled longer distances, it became unruly to carry stock, and so a form of currency was created. In China, small replicas of the goods to be bartered were forged in bronze. These were later reduced in size and made circular to be easier to carry.

In 600BC, the first currency was officially minted in Lydia, in modern-day Turkey. From this point – when the goods became separated from the coinage, it has shaped human ideas about money and wealth.

As a result, we attach emotion to money. Money may make us feel happy. Money may make us anxious. Money means something different to each of us. But really it is just a form of exchange.

The "Money = Success" Trap

Money has become equated with 'success'. This is a huge misconception. The purpose of life is not wealth creation, but enjoying it and achieving your 'true goals and purpose' – doing things that really matter to you and that you're passionate about.

Our time is poorly spent focusing on what isn't important. Things like paying bills and sacrificing our own enjoyment for the sake of saving. Much of the time, these are a by-product of not following our own passions and following someone else's – or society's – imposed goals and desires.

You can cut through all the noise about what 'success' really means and away from the false meanings, like fancy cars to a big home and a lavish lifestyle. These are not important unless you really love cars or houses.

What is important is doing what truly drives you.

When you are clear on this, you will be motivated to succeed and find your true passion.

This is the reason why so many people struggle to find happiness – chasing the wrong goal.

What money is *not*

Money is *not* security.
Money is *not* freedom.
Money is *not* worry.
Money is *not* good or evil.
Money is *none* of those things.
Freedom is freedom. Security is security. Worry is worry.
And money is just … money.

We've become used to connecting and associating one idea with another and making it conditional upon having money. That's not true at all.

As adults, we've learned to put far too much importance on money.

Adults aren't always right. If you want a healthier way to be about money, just look at how a child acts around money.

Think like a child, get rich quick

Imagine I gave you £10,000 and asked you to try and increase my investment in just two hours using trading. How would you feel? Nervous? Excited?

This is a perfect example of how differently children perceive money at a young age and how they don't let it affect their decisions and behaviours.

As part of our trading education and training business, my partner, Darren, runs a charity training course to show children how to trade. For one hour, he teaches children two simple trading strategies. They then have two hours to use those strategies on a demo account to see what they can do.

They start with a £10,000 account, and the goal is to make as much in those two hours as possible to win a prize.

If you've never experienced a room full of children trading, it's like nothing you've experienced before – the energy was incredible!

At the end of two hours, the first winner had made £1600, the second £1200, and the third £800. In just two hours!

If it was real money, I'm sure they would achieve the same results, because for these children it doesn't make any difference if it's real money or not. They were playing; they were laughing, one kid joked about how he managed to make £1000 in the first hour and almost lose it all in the second hour. Someone shorted Donald Trump's election bid, another sold EURUSD, and joked they could sell America.

It all felt like a game to them, and the energy was amazing.

Now contrast this with what you experience when you attend an adult live trading course. What do you think the energy is like there?

… Fear

… Stress

… Greed

… Anxiety.

Everyone is trying so hard to concentrate. It's serious.

There's no game element at all, and the energy is low. For the adults, money is serious business, and it's too important to treat as a game.

This is where it all goes wrong …

Think of this another way – in terms of sitting an exam.

If you come to an exam, and you think your whole life depends on it, is it going to make it easier for you to pass the exam or harder?

Harder, right? Of course, that's true.

If you are tense, nervous, and anxious, you struggle to perform. On the other hand, if you're relaxed and confident, you are more likely to perform well.

In the same way, if you put so much importance on money, attracting it becomes a struggle. Money is attracted to fun, lightness, creativity, confidence, and game. If you hold onto anxiety, fear, and worry, it only creates more obstacles for you.

The real reason why money is an issue (it's not really about money)

You see, all these problems – debt, lack of savings, struggling to make ends meet – are not the real problem.

They are the symptoms of a bigger problem. That problem is not dealing with how we feel about money or what we associate it with.

Remember my little history lesson on money? Money is just a form of exchange. Nothing more, nothing less. The problem is, we attach emotion.

For some people, money is abundant and offers an opportunity to do greater things. For many, though, money brings anxiety, fear, and worry. Thinking about money in the last example can suck the joy out of anything.

Money is like that. Some people give it the power to change how they feel about their life, situation, and themselves, but – and this is a huge but – it only works for a short time.

Money does not change who you are. You are you. It's true whether you are rolling in wealth or don't have two pennies to rub together.

The question is: how can one person feel so differently around money compared to another?

Simple. It comes back to our beliefs, virtues, and the way we see the world.

So here's the good news: until and unless you change

your limiting beliefs, you will always feel the same way about money and wealth. And here's the great news: you just need to get rid of your limiting beliefs to transform your financial reality!

If you've ever tried to change anything in your life, you probably know it is not as simple as just making the decision. There's sometimes a block, and there's often a very good reason why you can't shift it consciously.

Who cares about money, anyway? (or why you don't actually need money)

You don't really need money.

Like Jesus feeding the 5000, we can manifest anything we want instantly out of the energy of creation or unconditional love.

If you could do that, why would you need money?

Manifesting is our natural ability. Do you remember about your divinity? We can manifest everything.

Some of us just forgot who we are, our true creativity. Love is our true nature.

When people ask for money, they miss the point altogether.

When we can manifest a car or a house, why do we need money at all?

Your goal or your wish is the end game. Money is the means to get it.

When you want money, you can have it.

And there is one exercise I do at Money Magic workshops for students that reinforces this: the Money Rain. You can have a glimpse of it on my YouTube channel, you can find the link on my website www.prosperitycode.co.uk.

How to make it rain money

One of the most eye-opening experiences for students of my *Money Magic* course is the Money Rain.

The Money Rain is what it says: you experience £50,000 in crisp bank notes raining down upon you.

By experiencing the abundance of money falling on you, you become more aware how comfortable and accepting of it you are.

Few people will ever experience having £50,000 rained upon them.

How do you think you would feel?

(If you want to see it in action, go to my Facebook page to see videos of the Money Rain happening at https://www.facebook.com/ProsperExpert/)

Here's the really strange thing – as soon as I publish the date for the *Money Magic* course, the cash finds *me*.

At one course, I had a student bring £7000 in cash for my stock market trading course. Later the same day, my accountant stopped by and handed me over £20,000 in cash in the lift.

No one carries cash these days! I don't carry cash.

But when I plan a *Money Magic* seminar date, I don't even need to order it from the bank. It just arrives on cue. That's the power of manifestation.

How to start manifesting what you want

I was working with one man who wanted to manifest a dream home. There was a problem.

The picture that came to his mind when he thought of his dream home was so negative that it blocked his manifestation.

I asked him what happened, and he said he saw himself alone in that house and with no one to love.

If there is such an association with a manifestation, clearly, the person had negative beliefs around wealth. This man believed if he was wealthy, he would be alone, and his friends would struggle to accept him. Of course, he didn't realise this, as it was a subconscious belief: I can't be wealthy and happy. Which is not true, of course.

When you picture exactly what it is you want to manifest, make sure there is no negativity associated with it. If you don't feel comfortable with something, it could cause you to block your manifestation.

I worked with another client who was a gentleman with issues of sabotaging his success. When we did some work together, I realised his fear of success was associated with heights. He had a fear of being high up on a ladder. His belief was the higher he went, the more people he lost on the way, and the fewer friends and loved ones he had. Although he didn't come to me to work on his fear of heights, it was only then we discovered that here we were able to kill two birds with one stone. Back then, I used to live on the eighth floor of an apartment block. At the end of the session, we went out on the balcony, and he had no more fear of heights.

> "I have just attended Tatjana's Magic Money course.
> We explored a lot of new ideas and I was encouraged.
> People, who want to connect spirituality with money are
> extremely recommended to attend this course, I definitely
> will do it again."
>
> Joseph E.

Here's an exercise to help you manifest what you *really* want.

Exercise – 10 things to manifest

I would like you to write down 10 things that you want right now on a piece of paper or pad. But I want you to do it very quickly.

I always remind my students at seminars to use manifestations for absolutely everything. People often make the mistake of manifesting only the big stuff like a car or a dream home or a million in a bank account.

In fact, if you practice manifestation daily with relatively small things, you become better. And the more things you manifest, the stronger your faith will become.

How about manifesting yourself a nice breakfast or a wonderful dinner? How about manifesting a parking space or a taxi the moment you step out into the street? Or a bus as soon as you arrive at the bus stop?

Yes, you really can manifest anything.

Make sure you use this in every possible way for everything you can think of.

The reason I want you to practice this is so you don't load too much importance on to your manifestation. Remember what I wrote earlier about energy and lightness – the same is true here. When you are relaxed about manifesting, you will get things a lot easier and a lot quicker than expected. If you start with small things you get daily anyway – like dinner – you are unlikely to have any resistance. This will help you manifest the bigger stuff, if you still divide your wishes into small and big.

Start building your faith in your powers. Look at your list of 10 and try to really build a picture of each one, visualise on a daily basis, until it materialises in your life. Let's see how quickly you manifest each of these.

If you would like to learn advanced manifestation techniques, I cover this in far greater detail in the *Money Magic* course. To find out more, go to www.prosperitycode.co.uk .

Why some people find it hard to change

"She generally gave herself very good advice, (though she very seldom followed it)"

LEWIS CARROLL

Why we don't change ... even when we *really* want to

Every month, I run workshops and webinars teaching people what I'm showing you in this book. If you'd like to join me to learn how to use this, check out our next workshop here: www.prosperitycode.co.uk

Most people who come to my seminars either struggle with money, even though they have already done some self-development work, or are quite well off and are trying

to understand why they feel unfulfilled. I even work with celebrities that could be seen by many people as wealthy and having everything, but these 'lucky and chosen ones' also have issues to work on, and they want to know why they feel something is missing in their life.

Together, our goal is to break from behaviour patterns that don't serve us and remove limiting beliefs and acquire much-needed resources. This is the path to make money in a fun, easy way, and also enjoy life in the process.

This works for all aspects of our life, not just money.

Have you ever noticed that when your bank balance reaches a certain level, you get the urge to spend the surplus?

Or when you get fit and lose a few surplus pounds but feel the need to eat badly or stop exercising that causes you to go back to your old ways?

Or you keep ending up in the same kind of situations again and again, despite trying so hard to avoid them?

It feels like there is something else going on. Well, there is.

The reason we do this is explained by how our brain functions.

How to unblock core beliefs holding you back... in an instant!

Beliefs, blocks or traumas can be deeply rooted in your subconscious. They don't always reveal themselves straight away. Or they are hidden behind other beliefs.

It is important to discover what we call our 'core' beliefs. To do that, we need to look deep. There are prizes for guessing exactly what this means!

We use the process of Instant Transformation Technique (ITT) to keep pushing through the different layers of beliefs we have built up over the years to eventually discover the key belief that is driving many other beliefs. Unless and until you identify and uncover the most deeply held beliefs and thoughts in your subconscious, you will not create the kind of lasting change you want to your thoughts and behaviour around money and wealth.

The process is less like being an interrogator and more about asking the right questions to get what you want.

It can certainly be a bit unusual, when you first do it, but the results are profound.

You can do it on your own or with a professional. If you are particularly intuitive and good at reading your body and mind, you have a better chance of getting to the bottom of the issue faster.

The 'transformation' process is one of the most helpful techniques I use with my clients. If you're struggling to break through during the process, it is recommended that you go to an experienced practitioner, who will be able to look more deeply, than if you were alone.

What's *really* in charge of your behaviour?

Our mind is like an iceberg.

The conscious mind is the tip of the iceberg.

It is the part of which most people are aware of. We have conscious thoughts and believe these are what drives our decisions.

Think the conscious mind is everything that you are? Think your mind is in charge?

Wrong.

Scientists say that with our conscious mind, we use between 2–15% of our brain. That's how much power it has over our behaviour.

It is our subconscious that rules us. If you want to know who's really in charge, it's this guy.

Our subconscious is up to 98% of our awareness. It's the rest of the iceberg, hidden from view, but always there.

Some people are on autopilot most of the time, and it is the subconscious processes that allow us to survive each day.

We can deal with beliefs on a conscious level, but what is more powerful? The 2% conscious mind or the 98% subconscious. It's not even a contest!

Regardless of what you deal with on a conscious level, your subconscious will always be stronger.

You can't decide to stop breathing. You can't decide to stop digesting food or decide to stop your blood flowing around your body (unless you have very special training). Your subconscious rules you.

If the 98% subconscious is more of who we are than the tiny 2% conscious mind, what does this mean?

You might not truly know who you are.

OK, that may blow your mind!

But doesn't that explain why your behaviour doesn't always match your intention?

If you're not connected to your subconscious, you don't know what beliefs are ruling your life.

Here are a couple of examples.

Healthy eating – You know you need to eat healthily. Yet, some people don't. You know it on a conscious level. But some people still can't stop eating junk food or sweets. Even when some people put on weight or their doctor tells them that if they continue this way, they'll end up with diabetes, it still doesn't stop them. They can't quit. We're told changing behaviour requires a lot of willpower. We're told that you need strong willpower to quit smoking or drugs. These are common beliefs in the Western world.

Relationships – You have a fight with your partner. There are arguing and anger. When it ends, you know you need to apologise or say sorry straight after or the next day. But you don't. You find it hard to put aside your ego and say sorry. Your pride will not allow you to make the first move, even though you know it is the right thing to do, because you might believe that forgiveness is weakness and not strength. It rules you.

These are straightforward and obvious examples of when we know we need to do something better, but we don't have sufficient resources to do it.

Our conscious mind doesn't have the resources we need. The brain is just one small part of what we are, although we're led to believe it is everything we are. It isn't.

Humans cannot live without a heart or a liver, brain or lungs. We are a whole creature that needs everything in balance.

How beliefs shape your world

OK, we're going to have fun now!

Let me start by asking you a question: How many beliefs do you hold about money? How many of those beliefs are harmful or come from a place of fear?

Maybe you don't know or haven't thought about it before. Or have tried and come up with nothing?

When we really stop and analyse what we say and what we think, only then do we see how our beliefs about money shape our world. If we see the world, how it really is – of abundance and opportunity – we create success. However, if we distort the truth about what money or success is, we can see only scarcity and lack.

How many of the following beliefs have you heard? And, more importantly, how many of them do you agree with?

Before you continue, try this quick exercise to see whether you hold any beliefs about money. Don't turn the page until you have done this exercise.

EXERCISE: Your money beliefs

On a blank sheet of paper, write down as many beliefs about money that you personally hold or have heard from friends, family, or colleagues. Write down everything you can.

Now, look at your list. How many of the things you wrote are actually true? It's quite surprising when you look at it that you have so much nonsense about money in your mind, even if you don't consciously believe in them.

You're now ready to turn the page

If you completed the exercise on the following page, you probably found yourself writing a variation of one or more of the following statements.

"Money is bad … money is evil."
"I don't deserve to earn more money … "
"It's never enough … "
"No matter how hard I try, I never have enough money … "
"I always get cheated out of money … "
"I always end up sabotaging my success … "
"I never get above a certain sum of money in my bank account … "
"I always seem to spend everything I earn."
"I'm too comfortable to do anything about my situation."

If you find yourself saying or thinking any of these beliefs, therein lies the problem. It is quite common for most people in our society to hold limiting beliefs like these.

These beliefs are not just negative and disempowering; these beliefs affect us on a subconscious level, causing us to act in ways with and around money that don't benefit us.

For now, don't worry too much about holding these beliefs. Soon, I'll show you how to transform your belief systems by changing our neuron connections, I will show you that for every problem, there isn't just a solution, but an opportunity.

We can rephrase every point above with phrases that are empowering and not based on fear.

"I attract money even during my sleep … "
"Money works for me all the time … "
"I have more than enough … "
"It is in my power to get what I want … "
"I always have the motivation to achieve anything in life … "

For this exercise, go back to your original list and do precisely that. Rephrase every single belief as an empowering statement. Go on, do it now.

Why my illness returned

Two weeks after I received my very first instant healing, I realised that my illness started to return. It wasn't as severe as before, but I did still feel some discomfort. It turns out that the reason this illness returned was that I still enjoyed some benefit from having it.

That sounds strange, but it was true. When I was unwell, it was an excuse for me not to work, travel the world and meet all these wonderful healers and people with special powers.

Before I didn't know how to build healthy boundaries and how to say, "No." Without the illness, I thought I couldn't just allow myself to do what I wanted. I felt some kind of obligation when I was growing my business and bringing up my kids. Without this disease, I didn't allow myself to do what I wanted. Now I know what the problem was, but back then I didn't realise what was going on.

If you think consciously, you can probably relate to some people or yourself when you have deadlines or obligations to fulfil.

How many people randomly say, "Okay, I'm tired, I'm going to take a holiday …" or "I don't feel like working today, I'm going to get some rest"?

You feel like you need an excuse, like illness or some problem. Then the illness or emergency becomes a source of comfort because it allows you to gain a benefit.

You don't need to have a reason to take a rest!

It doesn't make any sense. If you think about it logically without any programmes running and taking yourself out of any patterns of beliefs that work or society holds, who says you can't take rest when you want? Why wouldn't you allow yourself to respect your boundaries and respect your body? If your body tells you it's tired, why don't you have some rest or go to sleep?

Next time you want to take some time for yourself for self-care or rest and relaxation, pay attention to the language you use. Do you feel you have to justify taking time to rest? Do you always give a reason why you're spending the day in bed or taking a few days off? There does not have to be an excuse for your behaviour.

The benefit of staying just as you are

"Now, Tatjana, you HAVE gone crazy," you may be saying! "How can any limiting beliefs or behaviours benefit me? It can't benefit me to be poor or irresponsible or self-sabotaging?"

Really?

Beliefs don't just hold us where we are. Our behaviours and actions serve us in a way of which we might not be aware.

It's always worth looking at yourself and analysing your behaviour to ask the question: how does this serve me? Even if it's a clearly negative behaviour that causes problems and drama, we may be getting something from it.

A good example is with a parent I met after an event in St Petersburg recently. She was at the event and was waiting for her young son. When he came along, she was straight onto him – "Did you get all your things?" "Did you pick everything up?" "Are you sure you've remembered?"

I said to her, "Why are you controlling him instead of giving him a cuddle?"

She responded: "Because he always forgets things."

"Yes, and why and how does that serve you?" I replied. "Why does he always forget things? He allows you to control him. Why do you need to control him?"

"Oh yeah, so I feel needed, I suppose," she replied.

And what is it for someone to feel needed? To feel loved.

She followed the chain of awareness and worked it out herself. The only reason he forgets things is so she could remind him. As soon as she stops controlling him, he will stop forgetting things. People play along for a particular reason that we want or need. As soon as that benefit is eliminated, the behaviour changes instantly.

3 steps to success

Before we go on, let me run you through the three steps to shift your beliefs and change your world.

Step #1 – Remove limiting beliefs and blocks (using Instant Transformation Technique ITT)

Step #2 – Add virtues and resources

Step #3 – Take action towards the goal you really want

Looks simple, doesn't it?

Well, you'll be surprised! That's where we start before moving onto the process using our brain, human intuition, and ITT to change how you feel about money, wealth and your life.

How to identify your beliefs

"You begin to fly when you let go of self-limiting beliefs"

BRIAN TRACY

What is a belief?

What I discovered in meditations during my soul-searching about beliefs is that we don't need *any*.

What we need is the highest truth about how things are and how the world works. Belief is what we think might be a fact or true, because we read or heard it from someone and agreed with that opinion or information about something, then it could be reinforced by hearing it again or getting some similar experience, but which might be very far from the truth. Therefore the fewer constructs, philosophies, beliefs, expectations, and other junk about the world we have in our mind, the easier it is to see, feel, hear the truth, and get desired results.

Some practices and methods talk about levels of beliefs, or that it is impossible to get rid of all beliefs in, say, one session. I do not see much truth in that.

This is a good example of how beliefs can affect our life.

We can pick up some beliefs from what parents tell us, what society tells us, and what school tells us or even teachers and gurus. We all have free will, and we decide what we believe and agree with and what not.

Let's take an example of three children brought up in the same family. The three children in the family are always told by their parents that they are hopeless and useless. I know, it's mean, isn't it? But let's just pretend for now.

Say, the first child believes what his parents say and completely gives up (he takes on board their belief). He stops studying because what's the point? He believes he is hopeless; he's no good. Maybe later in life, he ends up living on income support, or he starts drinking or taking drugs. Besides, that's a good excuse for how he's turned out. His parents told him that.

The second child also took on the belief, but he went in completely the opposite direction. He became an overachiever. He excelled at sports, brought home trophies and prizes, and always showed up by having great grades. He excelled just to prove to his parents that he is worthy, not for himself – and this is the crucial difference. There's nothing bad about overachieving. However, it depends on the motivation for doing it.

The third child didn't take on the belief of his parents. He really did live happily ever after.

The power of someone imposing their beliefs on you can be hard to deal with. In my seminars, I usually pick an unsuspecting person sat at the front of the room and start a conversation.

"You're looking a little pale," I say, looking as concerned as I possibly can. "Are you okay?"

The person who was usually looking absolutely fine up to that point usually starts touching their face and shaking their head.

"Yes," they say.

But then I start to insist.

"Really? Maybe it was a long day?"

Then their demeanour changes.

"Well, perhaps, I'm a little tired ..." they agree.

They're fine, of course.

I always do this. Every talk. And I do this to demonstrate a point:

YOU HAVE FREE WILL!

If you don't take anything else from this book, remember this is one of the really, really important things and write it down in big letters wherever you can.

You always have free will to either take on a belief or reject it.

Nobody can do anything about it. If somebody from today tells you:

"You don't want to do a stock market course. Everyone loses money in the stock market."

"You're never going to succeed in this business because nobody before you has ever done this in our family ... " or

"Oh, you don't look so good ... "

You now know what to say. Watch out for so-called 'wellwishers', who under the false pretence of caring for you, try to install negative beliefs that there is something wrong with you.

Beliefs may also be passed from our ancestors. These beliefs we see in our pineal gland in the brain. If you draw a line from your forehead to the back and from side to side, at the intersection of this line is the pineal gland.

Until the 1950s, scientists didn't know the function of the pineal gland. But, funnily enough, the ancient wise men always knew. They called it the 'Home of the Soul' because this is where one of our master cells is located. This is where we carry a lot of information and genetic codes.

Here's how it works in practice. Imagine that five generations ago in your family history, one of your ancestors left a huge inheritance, which your family members fought over and maybe even killed each other. The belief back then was formed that money was a curse of the family. You weren't there. You don't know about it. But your genetics carry that belief. No psychologist can see or tell you that. The clairvoyant ones can find it and see it in your DNA. This is how intense it can be.

There are even differences in beliefs and mindsets between countries and places you travel. Do you notice that by going to another country, you plug into a different reality and actually feel a new perspective?

If you go to Thailand, you feel very different than if you go to Russia. There is something in the air. You're the same person with the same thoughts, but you feel there is something you have not experienced before. This is what we call collective consciousness, which is like an atmosphere and where lots of beliefs come from. We sometimes connect to these beliefs from religions, society, and the whole culture of the country and might even think they are ours. What's interesting is that some religions tell us that love of money is evil. Yet they are richest organisations in the world. A bit of a contradiction, don't you think?

We also feel differently about actions and behaviours depending on where we are. For example, in India, if somebody suddenly goes into meditation, stops talking, and sits down where they are for days, it's perfectly normal. If that happens, people will notice, and they'll start taking care of the person – feeding them, moving them, if needed, and making sure they're safe. They know how much good this person's meditation is going to do for them, so they're happy to.

Try doing the same in London, however, and it would be a very different story. If you decided to sit down and start meditating in the middle of Trafalgar Square on a busy Saturday afternoon, what would people think?

Yes, they'd think you're crazy. So there are differences in perception of exactly the same situation.

Proof of meditation affecting peace

There were multiple studies done on the effects of meditation and Theta frequencies. I know of various groups of people who travelled to war zones and meditated for hours. During that time and for some time after, there was a noticeable decline in war and aggressive activity. You can look up some studies on influence of meditation here: http://www.worldpeacegroup. org/washington_crime_study.html.

There also studies showing the positive effect on our health from meditation, as well as how group prayer or meditation can also make water cleaner and more crystallised.

Garbage In, Garbage Out

I'm going to get all IT geeky with you, now. (Don't worry, I won't get *too* technical.)

There is a principle that applies perfectly to beliefs and the human brain. If you are familiar with programming, you'll recognise the term G.I.G.O., an abbreviation of "Garbage In, Garbage Out".

Our brain works exactly like a computer. Put a virus into a computer, and it is going to corrupt files and slow down or stall or even break down instead of functioning as it should.

When we feed negative thoughts and non-serving beliefs into our brain, the same happens. It is like a virus. Reality becomes distorted. You don't see opportunities when they appear, and you don't act in your best interests.

The key is to understand what is *really* going on. Understand how your brain works and how your beliefs shape your view of money, and you have the power to shift your thinking in ways you probably haven't experienced before.

Through the many seminars and workshops I run, I meet a lot of people. I have seen first-hand so many talented and intelligent people held back by their beliefs.

It is inspiring to help them pull and remove the non-serving beliefs and give them resources that allow them to prosper. (You can access all these resources and downloads from my website: www.prosperitycode.co.uk)

The crazy thing is I can almost guarantee you are holding onto a set of beliefs that are not originally your own. They may have been passed to you by your parents, ancestors, by society, or from someone else's perspective … but not your own. The problem is, these beliefs are now shaping how you think and feel about money, and they might be restricting you in your success.

Think of this book as an intuitive body scan. It is designed to help you see right inside yourself to identify beliefs causing problems in your life.

Once we have identified these limiting beliefs, I will show you how to replace these beliefs with the right resources that open up your thinking about your true potential.

What is belief work?

The act of identifying, removing, and replacing beliefs is what we call: belief work. To explain belief work, let's continue with the analogy of a computer.

Imagine your brain is a computer that performs certain functions.

For this, certain programmes are established (there are a lot of them!). Some programmes were established at birth, some were established by your parents and the environment in which you grew up. All these programmes together determine how you perceive the world and what you believe about how things are. These programmes determine your actions.

Some programmes are clearly visible, and it is easy to understand what functions they perform (they are on view on the desktop), but some programmes start automatically when a trigger occurs. You may not use them, and they only clutter up the working memory space and slow down the computer.

(If you have a Windows computer, you know what I mean!)

Also, some viruses can stop everything working or make it almost impossible to use your computer.

Belief work is like an anti-virus clean-up. By using it, programmes are found and removed that no longer serve you and are replaced with positive resources (helping the computer) to work even better and faster. By doing this process, we remove viruses and recognise and neutralise threats.

Of course, this is a very simplified principle of technology. But, effectively, belief or energy work is a method designed to help you get what you want and make life easier, simpler, and more fun and enjoyable.

Harmony and balance is a philosophy for life, and it can be really cool, once you know how to achieve it.

I tried lots of different methods and found some that work better than the others. Yet, they were all missing something: took a long time, or were too complicated to use, even if they seemed easy at first sight.

I like to simplify things, especially after removing the following beliefs: the harder things are, and the more effort you put into something, the more valuable they are; easy things cannot be exciting and interesting.

After working as a coach for a while, I realised things don't need to be complicated in order to be effective, so I started questioning how truthful each technique was and discovered something interesting. Working with the energy of creation or unconditional love, I asked the question: what is a belief, and is it useful to have them?

After asking The Creator, I received the answer. No. We don't need beliefs. We need true knowledge about how things are and how to do, get, or create things and a variety of virtues to make it more interesting.

Some methods suggest removing negative beliefs and substituting them with positive beliefs. However, in conversations with The Creator, I discovered that instead of a belief, it is much better to download a virtue that will help you with a particular task.

Let's look at an example. Consider a man who wants to buy his own apartment. No matter how much he works, he struggles to save enough to buy a property.

He saves and tries to earn more. All his thoughts and intentions go towards the realisation of this goal, yet he still cannot buy an apartment.

His money ends up going on daily or unexpected expenses. The reasons may be many, but the fact remains that no matter how hard he tries, what he desires eludes him. The reasons may be blocks and beliefs that hinder the manifestation of his desire, of which he may not even be aware.

With belief work – in some techniques – a practitioner scans a person for such blocks and installations, identifies them, and removes inefficient installations and programmes. The removal of these blocks and inefficient beliefs allows the person to finally reach their goals since they are no longer hampered by restraining factors.

Of course, this doesn't mean that after the practitioner's work, there won't be a need to do anything else. Belief work is not a Magic Pill.

But, using this technique in your life, achieving your desires is faster, easier, and undoubtedly, more fun and enjoyable without all the internal resistance. I learnt many different methods, modalities, and meditation techniques and discovered in the process a straightforward and accessible method that I want to share with you. I called it ITT (Instant Transformations Technique).

Let's go back to the computer analogy again.

For example, you are writing an article or paper. You have a lot of programmes running on your computer, so the text application doesn't have enough memory to function. You type a letter and wait for a few minutes until the change is reflected upon the screen. You are impatient and angry. Yet, the computer does not start working faster.

As soon as you close unnecessary files and programmes and clean your computer from viruses, you can work quickly, effectively, and it's a much more enjoyable experience.

That's why it is useful to clear non-serving beliefs. Removing these beliefs helps you achieve what you desire, easily and efficiently.

Why you don't need to give up anything for money

You don't have to give up anything. It's a common belief that you have to give up something in exchange to get something else. It's just not true.

(Honestly, have you ever felt this to be true in your life? Most people have. The difference between them and you is that today you stop!)

You can learn so much from helping others.

I had one gentleman on my seminar, who had a bankruptcy case going on in court. This issue had been going on for a few months around his properties. He told me in confidence that things started going wrong for him a few years back. He had been losing one business after another, and he didn't understand what the problem was or why it was happening.

We explored his past, and he later revealed he had spent many years studying with a guru in India.

Ten years earlier, when he started seeing this guru, the guru was willing to teach him, but he said he would take something in return for his effort.

The man agreed to this because he wasn't exactly sure what this guru was asking him. It was only later on during our conversation he realised what he had given up – his money. The contract or the obligation that was created between them was giving up money for knowledge.

We completed and cleared this trade of money in exchange for knowledge and wisdom – a sacrifice he was prepared to make at that stage – and finished the session. Later, he had a message from his lawyer with great news: an investor had come in and saved his business.

The common belief is that to get something, you have to give something or that "there is no such thing as a free lunch" or "there is only free cheese in a mousetrap." You have to sacrifice something. That's the cost. There's just one issue with that. It's not the highest truth of the universe. You don't have to give up anything. Anything you ask or manifest from unconditional love is unconditional!

The myth of 'sacrifice'

"You can't have a family and a career."
"You can't build a business and take too many days off."
"You can't eat what you want and be healthy."

How many of these have you heard?

They're taken as the gospel truth by so many people. How true are these, really?

It's common to hear people talk about sacrifice when it comes to money. It's a narrative that's very popular, both among successful people and with those who coach others for a living.

Being successful is all about sacrifice, we're told. You have to make sacrifices today to reap the fruit of your hard work in the future. Or the most nonsense advice I have come across: focus on one thing to master it or to succeed.

When you truly understand what having an abundant mindset is, you will see: there is no sacrifice. There is no need to give up things that are important to you, just because you want to make money and become wealthy and successful. You don't have to limit yourself.

To demonstrate the truth of this, I have my students take part in an exercise when they attend my wealth and mindset workshops.

It's certainly worth doing this now as it will most likely highlight some valuable insights into your beliefs around money. Don't turn over the page until you've completed this exercise to get the full effect.

EXERCISE – Money can't buy

For this exercise, find a piece of paper or a page in a journal and draw a line down the middle to create two columns.

To begin with, write down on one side of the paper all the things that you want and that, you believe, money can buy.

When you have completed that list, on the other side of the paper, list all the things you want, but which, you believe, money cannot buy.

You should now have two lists. Now turn over the page.

Things I want and can buy	**Things I want and cannot buy for money.**

There is a pretty standard range of things that people write on the 'money can't buy' list. These include:

... Love
... Friendship
... Happiness
... Health

These are common things we're told money can't buy.

Now rephrase all the items in the 'money can't buy' list to explain how money *could* help you achieve those things. For example, you can't buy good health, but you can get the best medical care or work with the best healers. You have the money and can afford it.

If you believe money cannot make somebody love or like you, you can write how you can make that person happier by using money. How you can be creative with money, so they don't feel that you're trying to buy them, but you can make them feel loved with gifts of flowers or dream holidays? How you can create an amazing experience for them? How you can be generous without making them feel 'bought'?

It usually turns out that there isn't a single thing that 'money can't buy'.

This exercise identifies blocks against what people say money can't buy. These are what we call 'contracts', conditions or sacrifice, when you trade one thing for another, instead of having both.

'Contracts' – the real reason you're struggling to get what you want

Contracts or sacrifices are when we make an exchange. A contract is a trade or swapping something we want for another thing in our lives. Contracts are very damaging and are what hold you back. And that's why we need to remove them from your life!

Maybe someone has exchanged love for money, and that's

why they have lots of money but are not happy with their partners. Or they have a programme that, at some stage in their life, they felt they had to sacrifice friendship to become successful financially.

All the things identified as things that money can't buy will be a programme of sacrifice.

It is an erroneous belief and it would be a relief to eliminate it. The concept of abundance is that you can have everything you want at the same time. You never have to sacrifice anything.

Many people have been led to believe that sacrifice is essential or good. In religion, for example, sacrifice is seen as a virtue when it is actually a vice. It is a violation of your boundaries and disrespect of yourself. And, obviously, there is not much self-love if you do something for others that could harm you or you really don't like or even hate.

This is a bitter pill to swallow. Hearing that making a sacrifice is a vice goes against so much of our existing programming. It's a story that's entrenched in our thinking, unfortunately.

Let me repeat: it is not true. It is a very harmful belief that causes so much damage.

The reason why some people struggle to be successful, no matter how hard they try, is this belief in the background. They don't want to become successful because they believe they have to miss out on their time, their loved ones, fun, friendship, happiness, or everything to get what they really want. As soon as they start to experience some success, they start to sabotage it because they don't want to lose what they've got if they're already quite happy and comfortable.

How many times have we seen this play out in our own lives or lives of people we know?

Pretty much 99.9% of people in the Western world believe it. Even practitioners of many spiritual practices who don't believe it consciously may still hold the belief on another level.

How to discover your limiting beliefs

"But ... but ... but I don't think I have any limiting beliefs."

Trust me, that's what every person with limiting beliefs says!

The truth is, I haven't met a person yet who didn't have beliefs that were restrictive in some shape or form. You have limiting beliefs. Yes, you do. I still have limiting beliefs. The point is to be moving into a highly resourceful state, rather than out of it.

When we operate from fear, greed, anger, and limitation, it hurts us. When we operate from a space of trust, faith, abundance, joy, and happiness, it helps us. How do we get more of that!

Getting into a place of happiness is all about shifting from talking about sacrifice and "must" and "having to do" things towards the mindset of "I want" and "I love doing."

You can discover all in your language ... so let's look at YOUR language right now.

Beware ... your words reveal you

What you say reveals everything about your beliefs. Words really aren't cheap! The words you use describe your universe.

To demonstrate here's a quick test. Do you find yourself saying any of the following phrases ...?

"I must do this ... "
"I have to do this ... "
"I should do this ... "
"I need to do this ... "

When you uncover your unconscious beliefs, you discover it comes through in your language as well. You see, people speak in programmes. People speak their belief systems. It may seem you're just using a figure of speech or a form of words. Those words say everything about how you see yourself and the world around you.

I achieved things because I thought that is what you're supposed to do. We do things for others or put our own needs aside. Going back to the exercise on listing 100 things, it's a case of being able to truly know the wishes you have written down on that list are things you want, rather than things you're supposed to want or supposed to do.

When we remove limiting beliefs and replace them with the highest truth that serves you, your language changes to:

"I want to do this ... "
"I love to do this ... "
"I chose to do this ... "

Look at what difference it makes when you use language that comes from an empowering place. It sounds inspiring and strong with every word.

These programmes reveal themselves through speech, although they operate beneath the surface.

You can tell the same story to two people, and both could come to completely different conclusions. Same situation, same story, different conclusion. You can present someone with exactly the same facts, but how they see the world dictates the outcome of that situation.

People will quite often assume something after you talk to them, which isn't necessarily what you meant. But their brain is wired a particular way with a programme that will either serve them or harm them.

This is also how people see an opportunity. One person can see one situation and notice it filled with possibilities. Another person can look at the same situation and see nothing; they cannot understand how or what they can apply to their own life.

When I look at my own life and the journey, I realise how my outlook on life has served me. I've not been lucky to have opportunities and possibilities fall in my lap. By having the right resources that helped me, I created my opportunities – and you will, too.

How to test your beliefs

One of the most powerful ways to test your beliefs is through a process called muscle testing.

Muscle testing works on the basis that for truth and lies, you will receive different responses from your body. On truth, muscle response will be stronger than on lies.

Here's a classic test method you can do on your own:

1. Stand up with your feet parallel to each other, shoulder-width apart.
2. Stand straight, relaxed with your eyes closed.
3. First, say something which is definitely true, such as "My name is …" and say your name to test the truth. If it is true, you will lean forward. (Hopefully, it is!)
4. Then say something that is definitely not true, such as "My name is Michael" (unless your name is Michael, in which case say something else!) to test a lie. If it is a lie, you will lean backwards.
5. Do not try to lean either way deliberately, just let your body give you a signal.

So, now you see how the body responds to different statements.

I always work on simplifying things and making them more accessible and easy. So on my website, you can find an easier way of testing your beliefs, wherever you are and whether you can stand up or not at www.prosperitycode.co.uk .

Muscle testing works on the principle that for truth, the muscle responses is stronger. For lies, the muscle response is weaker. Lying is stress for the body. When faced with a statement that is not true, the muscles weaken.

To do muscle testing, it helps to have another person with you or a practitioner with you to help test the beliefs.

1. Sit or stand straight and relaxed with your arm held out to the side.
2. The other person will try to push down on your arms to test the muscle response to see whether a belief is a truth or a lie.
3. Now read out a series of statements about money while the other person is pushing down on your arms. If your arms remain strong, the statement is true. If your arms feel weak, and the other person can push them down, the statement is a lie.
4. Start with the "My name is ..." test you did in the 'sway' test before to test you're getting the truth and lie responses to the right questions.
5. Then read through a list of beliefs to test each one.

Here are some programmes to get started:

- *I love money.*
- *I hate money.*
- *Money is betrayal.*
- *If I am a millionaire, I will become a bad person*
- *Money spoils me*
- *Money is dangerous*
- *Money is fear*
- *Money is a curse/blessing*
- *Money is spiritual*
- *Money is evil/root of all evil*
- *Money is love*
- *Money is pointless*
- *I am in debt*
- *I owe everyone*
- *Everyone owes me*
- *I want money*
- *I need money*
- *Money harms spirituality*
- *Money harms friendship*

- *Money excludes happiness*
- *Money obstructs connection with God*
- *I am afraid of money*
- *I am afraid of big money*
- *Money is boring*
- *Money is control*
- *Money exists*
- *I am a victim of money*
- *I want to get rid of money*
- *I only need enough money to survive*
- *Money is freedom*
- *Money is abundance*
- *I have to reject financial abundance*
- *I have vows of asceticism*
- *I have a blessing for poverty*
- *I am allowed to have money*
- *I need permission to be rich*
- *I accept money*
- *I am worthy of money*
- *Money is beneath me*
- *I depend on money*
- *I serve money*
- *Other people are responsible for creating money for me*
- *It is possible for me to be a millionaire*
- *I hate paying taxes*
- *I sacrifice my money for others*
- *I try to be modest with what I take for me, so it is enough for everyone*
- *I have to share my abundance with others*
- *I have a blessing to be free from money*
- *I understand that money is spiritual and divine and is a manifestation of the creator*
- *I know how to create money for me*
- *I mistake money for a vice*
- *Money influences all areas of my life in a positive way*
- *Money is the curse for me*

- *Money divides people*
- *If I am rich, I will die*
- *I control my money*
- *I am responsible for my finances*
- *Abundance is dangerous*
- *Money ruins lives*

Just by doing muscle testing, you can discover a lot of surprising things about money and wealth in particular.

You can have conflicting beliefs, for example, stating you're rich and you're poor at the same time. How is this possible? It's possible because different beliefs can come from different experiences. Maybe your ancestors believed they were poor and you believe, now, that you are rich. It's hard to understand how you could hold both beliefs until you realise it's not your belief, but it comes from your ancestor – so if you connect to their collective consciousness, your subconscious or your DNA will carry it.

That's why it helps to test if a belief is yours, your mother's or your father's or if it comes from the collective consciousness and belief system of a whole country or religion.

There's only one trick to remember. You have to ask the right questions. If you ask the wrong question, you will get wrong answers or answers you don't need or aren't helpful.

As with many things, it's not always about the answer. It's about asking the right question.

I can help you get started. Go to my website www.prosperitycode.co.uk to download a bigger list of beliefs you can use to get started with muscle testing.

The African tribe subconscious money test

Imagine I put £100 in front of you right now. How would you feel?

OK, I bet pretty much anyone in our culture will feel comfortable around £100.

But how would you feel around this ... a billion pounds or dollars or, even better, your billion pounds or dollars?

Would you be comfortable? Or would it be totally out of your comfort zone?

People aren't aware they have subconscious blocks that are not allowing money into their lives. And there's an ancient technique learned from African tribes, which helps uncover and change these blocks.

It's called Constellation Work, and it is used to help tribespeople solve problems.

When they had a problem, they would do a search through their ancestral tree and see where the problem came from.

It's a technique you can do yourself to see where a problem comes from.

There are certain laws of the universe that allow you to experience whatever someone else experienced. That other something doesn't even have to be a living person. Or it can be an object, like 'money'. (OK, if it sounds a little odd, I get it but give it a chance, it's really effective!)

To do the exercise, take an object which doesn't carry a lot of information (so not a book or computer).

Let's use a pillow for this example.

You nominate the pillow as you and you nominate yourself as your money (or anything else you want to work with).

Next, you move very slowly either away or towards the pillow (which you've imagined is you). As you do this, you will literally feel what it feels like to be around you for that object or person.

If you're struggling with finances, you may feel some kind of resistance if you get closer. So that will be a programme: I resist my money.

In this case, a person is not allowing money into their life. By nominating an object to be them and themselves as money, they feel what their money feels like to be around them.

You can switch it around, too. You release the pillow from the obligation to be you and then nominate your pillow as money and you back to being yourself. Then move around very slowly away from and closer to the pillow to experience from a different angle what you feel like around money.

It's funny how this works, isn't it? You can really experience different feelings when you move towards money and get a sense of any resistance or any other emotions.

Working with beliefs using Instant Transformation Technique

How quickly do you want to change?

If you've already done some belief work, excellent!

You're further ahead than most people, who aren't even aware their beliefs could shape their decisions and behaviours.

I can show you how to do this more efficiently and quickly. Some healers don't believe they can remove all beliefs in one or two sessions. I know you can because The Creator told me so.

Many modalities and methods do work to help you change your beliefs. If you've worked on self-development, you maybe already understand the world is abundant, and anything is possible. It really is. The limitation of some methods, though, that they may require lots of sessions over a long time, they rely on a healer's ability to read beliefs and situations, and some can be hard and not particularly user-friendly. To do the transformation properly, we need to look into our conscious and subconscious to make a real change.

The question is, how efficiently and effectively do all these methods remove a belief and replace it with something that truly serves you?

When you change a belief only on a conscious level, you're not removing it. All methods that focus on the mind will have particular limitations. People are a lot more than what we see with our eyes in front of us.

It is far more effective to use a method that allows you to access both your conscious and subconscious to perform real transformation.

Why the Instant Transformation Technique is the future

Twenty years ago, if you asked someone what Neuro-Linguistic Programming (NLP) was, they wouldn't be able to tell you. Look how big that has become!

Now, if you do sales presentations and you're not using NLP, you're seen as being behind the curve.

Today, using the Instant Transformation Technique (ITT) is the future. If you're not using this modality, you're going to fall behind.

Everyone at the cutting edge of business and science understands the importance of this knowledge. Nearly all Fortune 500 companies use the science behind theta waves to improve the success and performance of their management, including Google, AOL, Apple, and Salesforce. The application of theta waves is also widely used in the military, by NASA and the Russian space programme.

This may seem like something from TV, like *Fringe* or *The X-Files*. But only now are we beginning to understand the full potential of the human using intuition and energy of creation.

Shocking my massage therapist (accidentally)

After I discovered instant transformations, I experienced many more situations with instant healing. People around me experienced it too.

If I was having a manicure or a massage for a couple of hours, I would call a healer, and we would do a healing session over the phone. This could focus on anything from conflicts, court cases, money, health or relationship issues, anything that needed attention at the time.

During one healing session, while I was having a massage, I experienced a flash of light and instant healing again.

My massage therapist jumped in the air and shouted, "What was that? Did you just switch on the light?"

"No, I'm just lying here," I said, but she kept asking me about what had happened.

"I want to know about this," she said.

This is how it has been ever since. Many people who learnt this transformation technique have experienced this and wanted to know more. As a healer, I now work with clients to instantly change their beliefs and download much needed resources that work for them.

How I spread my transformation message without really doing anything)

"If you build it, they will come ..." is the line from the movie, *Field of Dreams* that talks about taking a leap of faith. Well, I did it too, and it proved right.

When I ran my first course, I never had to advertise to get people to join me. I wasn't like those annoying MLM marketing people who constantly try to keep talking about their products all the time, whether you want to hear about them or not. It was the opposite.

People around me saw the changes in me through my transformation work, and they wanted to know about it. They wanted to see how I went from the condition I was in and transformed into who I was a few months later.

As I wrote early, at one stage, my weight was down to 50 kilograms, which is terribly skinny when you're 180 centimetres tall. I was literally half the person I used to be. It wasn't a pretty sight, and people were worried about me.

So my first course was attended by people who had literally seen the change in me. When their friends, family, and colleagues started to see results in them, word spread. More and more people came to my seminars looking for help achieving their goals, removing stress from their lives, and living in a happier, more fulfilling way.

The process of ITT can help in all areas of life, including money and wealth. Here are some examples of how I've worked with clients:

Health – one celebrity client came to me for a session to work very specifically on his hay fever allergy. I personally witnessed an instant healing when working on the allergy. When I looked into the face of this person, I saw a lot of internal fight going on in his body. It was a normal and completely natural programme of the immune system fighting the harmful stuff in his body, but the programme was blown out of all proportions. I received the message from The Creator to teach the immune system to know the difference between harmful bacteria and pollen. Once the work was done and the download completed, I witnessed a flash of light and knew the job was completed. The person was free of hay fever.

Here is his testimonial:

"I had hay fever and spent 20 years visiting the world's top experts trying to cure it. Just one session with Tania and it was gone. I was more than amazed at how powerful these techniques are. Everyone should read this book and use the techniques, as it can transform any area of life where you want change."

Darren W

It's not always instant healing. I worked with one case of someone with cancer really early on in my healing career. My teacher got an urgent request for help with someone who was in the late stages of cancer. I was at the seminar learning about issues – but out of 30 healers, no one wanted to take on this case, so I did. I had no expectations at that stage, so I hoped I could offer some benefit. The client had a few sessions where we worked on her beliefs and issues. She held a lot of resentment towards men and had issues with forgiveness and acceptance. It was a more gradual process, but she got well, and now five years later, she's recovered from her breast cancer.

Wealth and success – one lady I worked with came to a *Money Magic* seminar, where we worked on an issue around success. She had put down a deposit on a property off-plan, and the building site was frozen for a few years. It was so long ago for her that she gave up and thought she had lost all her money because the project never seemed to finish. When we worked on this issue, we tried to discover what was sabotaging her success. It turned out she always put money into projects that stopped and stalled. It was her reality. So we did ITT transformation work, and later that day, she received a text from the developer to tell her she could come and view her new apartment during the week. She thought nothing would come out of that project, and after the news, she was jumping up and down overjoyed that it finally came through.

Love and relationships – one particular case was a woman who called me and was desperate. She told me she had a court case with her husband the next day, who wanted to take her children away. He hadn't paid child support for two years, and he wasn't really interested in seeing the kids – he was only doing this to get back at her.

We did a session together, and it was mainly focused around her trying to be so strong that she wouldn't accept any help from her partner because she thought it would be a sign of weakness. She drove him away by trying to do everything herself. When she realised, she also revealed her parents were always overprotective. Their motivation wasn't to control her but to take care of her and love her. She let go of her issues around flexibility, femininity, and forgiveness. She called me the next day and said her husband signed the papers all on her terms. He paid all the child support and had suggested going shopping together for the kids. She was extremely happy with the outcome.

So, as you can see, there are different ways Instant Transformation TechniqueITT can help in various areas of your life.

But, it's important to add that transformations aren't just for people with problems or people who find themselves in a desperate situation. Many clients who book sessions with me are extremely successful, have a high income, and don't have a single problem. So why do they want to work with me?

Some people want to gain a greater understanding of who they are by asking The Creator of All That Is about consciousness, the universe, and the highest truth, their purpose in life and divine timing. They want to explore new avenues in life, new roles, and find new things they want to try.

You don't need to be looking to heal anything to experience wonderful transformation. You may simply be looking to explore and find inspiration.

The discovery of divine connection has given me both the ability to transform myself and help others and understand why all these things happened. By understanding how the human brain works, how belief patterns subconsciously influence our behaviour and how to reconnect with our intuition, I worked out Instant Transformation TechniqueITT that offers a path to an easier and happier way of creating the life that you want.

The Placebo Effect and the power of faith

It is not my intention in any way to persuade you that ITT is for you. That isn't the purpose of this book.

If you're already sceptical about whether this could work, consider The Placebo Effect.

You may have heard about The Placebo Effect, which is unfairly viewed negatively by the medical establishment.

This effect is where the brain convinces the body to heal through the power of faith rather than because of some chemical interaction.

We've been led to believe by the scientific establishment that a placebo has a negative connotation, but studies show there is real backing for the value of The Placebo Effect in changing our physiology.

With instant healing using different modalities, the same part of the brain is activated as when a person is healed through the use of a placebo pill. In basic terms, a placebo is a scientific term for faith. If a person truly believes they will get well, it sets all the body mechanisms in motion to support the process. When we perform a transformation using ITT, faith is one of the ingredients.

The suggestion that a placebo is in some way not real or false does not take into account the changes it can bring to the body and mind through the power of love and faith. If you believe something is working, it works!

The Placebo Effect is real, it is positive, and it is a highly valuable tool we can use to change how we feel physically, emotionally, and spiritually. And it has no negative side effects! When you use ITT, you tap into the power of true faith.

The 'secret' to Instant Transformations (the mystery inside your head)

What do the military and secret services, Russian space programs, the leading Fortune 500 companies know that we don't? They understand and are already tapping into the power of our brain to function on different frequencies.

Let me introduce you to one of the most fascinating things you're ever likely to meet ... your brain.

Now you may think you know all about your brain. It is inside your head, after all. But your brain isn't quite as well known to you as you may believe.

In fact, we know less about the brain than we do about things like space. One of the greatest mysteries still to be discovered in the world is what really happens in a human brain.

Our brain operates in various different states, and each of them facilitates a specific ability.

Our mind can function in different brain waves and frequencies. We create our own world and future and turn our thoughts into reality.

By understanding who we are and how our brain works, we can access our subconscious mind, tap into it, and remove beliefs, traumas, and blocks that are in the way of accepting success and abundance.

To understand how to do this, we first need to know how the brain works.

There are different brain waves, named after Greek letters. Each state produces a different type of activity which accesses a different aspect of our abilities.

For most people, our natural state is what is called Beta state. Here are all the states of the brain (that we currently know of):

Beta – The Waking State
The beta state is when we work and do everyday chores. The brain functions at a frequency 14–30 cycles per second.

Alpha – The Dream State

Alpha is a little bit like a dream state. It's slower – 7–14 cycles per second – and this is the space where Reiki masters work from. If you've not heard of Reiki before, it is a common healing technique that accesses alpha waves. Practitioners of the Silva method also use alpha waves.

Alpha waves are the bridge between the conscious and subconscious mind. People who wake up in the morning and don't remember their dreams don't spend enough time in Alpha state. Basically, they don't dream enough; they've become too sceptical. Dream more, and you will improve your sleep, memory, and IQ.

Another way to access Alpha state is through visualisation. Imagine that you're standing on a beach and watching the sunset. You hear the sounds of the waves. You feel the warmth on your face. As soon as you start visualising, your brain instantly switches to Alpha. It's a dream-like state that is a borderline between waking state and sleeping state. (If you suffer from insomnia or have trouble sleeping, see Theta meditation instead, below).

Theta – Connecting with the Subconscious

Theta waves are much slower, with a frequency of 4–7 cycles per second. Most people experience Theta state when sleeping. If you use certain practices, you can achieve this state while being awake.

When we do transformation work, we can access Theta state for deeper intuition. Theta state is that moment just before you fall asleep and just as you awake from a deep sleep. That's why, when I'm teaching people, they often report feeling quite sleepy. Fortunately, that's not because I'm boring (or at least I hope not!), but because I teach in Theta and this automatically puts others into a Theta state. It could be described as a pleasant, intuitive, and empathic state. Of course, people who are not used to this can often just fall asleep while sitting in my seminars.

Accessing the Theta state is the way to your subconscious. And it allows us to work on our beliefs more efficiently.

We do all readings in any state, but in Theta state, some people find it easier to connect with their intuition. It is a wonderful feeling being in Theta. You feel more centred, calmer, and nothing can stress you out.

Since I learned this technique, boredom simply doesn't exist for me. On one 17-hour flight to Peru, I just sat on the plane and decided to do some Theta meditation and some healing. Seventeen hours later, I open my eyes to find we're landing. "Oh my God," I thought. "I haven't even had time to watch one film!"

When you learn to access Theta state, you don't need entertainments, you don't need your iPad or your phone, and you don't need seminars, teachers or books anymore. You can get your information feed directly from the source. (We'll talk about direct knowledge later on.)

Delta – Deep Sleep State

Delta is very, very deep sleep, hypnosis, or coma state. Have you ever experienced the situation when you're sleeping and the phone rings and you know exactly who is calling you? Basically, at this frequency, you can experience telepathy. Go to Delta, and you're able to read everyone's thoughts. Although this is supposed to be something from *X-Files* or *X-Men*, this 'superhuman' ability is really a human ability. Reading thoughts is your natural ability and your birth-right. You just need to know how to tap into the state.

On a physiological level, Delta deep sleep is beneficial for healing and regeneration, which is why a lack of sleep causes so many problems for some people.

Gamma – The Miracle State

Gamma is an amazing state. It has much faster brain waves, from 30–5000 cycles per second.

When you are learning, like now or when you're doing a course, you would have been in Gamma state because your brain is working fast processing information.

When we access the elusive Gamma state, this is when miracles happen. We can also access it to get certain results. This is the zone of superhumans, instant healings, and the power of positive thinking.

Have you ever been in a life-threatening situation, when you have to make decisions really quickly, like in a split second? In those moments, it suddenly feels like everything slows down, and you feel on top of the world, and you know exactly what to do. This is the brain wave that our mind accesses when the survival instinct kicks in.

You can see this in action in lots of places. You've probably read stories somewhere on the internet or watched on YouTube videos about a mother single-handedly lifting a truck to save her child. Why? She accessed her state of emergency. She just had to do it. She didn't have time to think if the truck was heavy – it probably weighed a few tonnes – she just did it. Did she bend the law of gravity? Did she gain superhuman strength? The story doesn't say, but possibly all the above. What actually happened: she accessed this magical state and did what she had to do.

Now, you understand some of the different states of the brain, and I hope you can see the importance of learning how to use it to the full potential and to our advantage. While teaching you the Instant Transformation Technique, I will show you how to access different frequencies and make changes in your beliefs and subconscious in order to create lasting change. And the best thing is it is easy, simple, and fun.

How to use the Instant Transformation Technique to remove beliefs and unleash your new future

I'm going to take you through the ITT process.

With the exercises so far, we have identified limiting beliefs and beliefs that don't serve you. Now through the ITT process, we can remove those beliefs and replace them with virtues.

Why should you not change a belief for another belief?

Using this process, once we have removed the belief, we can replace it with something helpful. Some modalities suggest replacing a limiting belief for another belief, albeit one that is not limiting. Yet there is a problem with this.

A belief is set, and it is not the highest truth, so it can affect you in a way you don't expect yet. Therefore, rather than swap one issue for another, it is better to replace beliefs with virtues that will be a resource for you, rather than a burden.

Why I don't give money to beggars

OK, so this sounds a *little* controversial, but this is really a story about being a victim. One experience made me realise what happens when you try to help people who don't want a true solution; they just want your money or something else.

When I was still stuck in my lean early years in London, I found a job in a sandwich bar for £2.50 per hour – which was terribly low even back then. There was an upside, though. I could eat as much as I liked.

(As you discovered, with my appetite, that *really* worked in my favour!)

One evening on my way to the station, I walked past a homeless person who called out to me and asked for money.

Now, this was a very unusual experience for me. In the whole time of being in the Soviet Union, I never met a homeless person. Homelessness didn't exist.

Like any decent person, I was saddened by what I saw. I wanted to help him with his situation.

"Hello, my name is Tania ..." I explained that I did not have money, but I could help him find a job, even if he didn't have any documents or an address. I reassured him with compassion that this was not a problem.

What I didn't expect was his response.

He just looked at me with anger in his eyes and spat out the words: "I just want money, you stupid bitch!"

I couldn't believe it. I had offered to help the homeless guy find work, and he was throwing it back in my face.

This incident made me realise that many people, who find themselves in their current situation, don't want solutions.

After this incident, I've never paid any attention to people asking for handouts of money. I do not give money for nothing, although I like donating a £5 or £10 note to a busker if I enjoy their music.

For a while after this situation, I came across many people, who loudly complained about their plight. They always spoke about how hard life was for them.

In each case, I willingly offered to help them with work or whatever their issues were. Guess what? Nobody *ever* accepted the help I was offering.

Finally, it dawned on me.

Many people are satisfied with their life, whatever it may be. And it is not painful enough for them to do anything about it.

Seriously, try offering real help to a victim and see how hard they try to wriggle out of making a change if it means they may have to give up their victimhood. It's comfortable for them. Why change if you can just whine about how bad things are?

The point I'm making is this. You create your reality, and you are the only person responsible for it and who can uncreate it.

People who play victims often want to stay that way. They live it, and it is too uncomfortable for a victim to let go of their label.

The power of virtues

To understand what is a virtue, it helps to know the difference between a virtue and a vice and also a skill, feeling, or something else.

Exercise – Virtue or vice?

Below is the list, please sort them into virtues on one side, vices on the other.

Compassion, Beauty, Pride, Sacrifice, Suffering, Pain, Love, Communication, Interaction, Fun, Playfulness, Humbleness, Religion, Faith, God, Truth, Kindness, Health, Healing, Heaviness, Lightness, Grace, Knowledge, Information, Trust, Joy, Courage, Arrogance, Humility, Loyalty, Power, Strength, Obedience, Flexibility, Cooking, Exercise, Pleasure, Sadness, Orgazmicity, Hardworking, Stubbornness, Determination.

What did you get? Was it hard to know the difference or easy?
Find the right answers here www.prosperitycode.co.uk .

So what is a virtue?

I looked up a dictionary suggestion for meaning of this word and was not satisfied, so had to come up with my own. A virtue is an energy with high vibrational qualities, which creates positive interaction with everything that is. When you feel it and manifest in your life, it is helpful and kind for you and everyone around you, and it feels good. When virtues show up, it is a win–win situation.

Another suggestion of definition of virtue is: perception of reality for what it really is in a truthful way.

Vices, on the other hand are harmful and are a means to achieve something through compromise due to lack of all needed resources. For example, sacrifice is sometimes thought to be a virtue but isn't. If you sacrifice, short-term, it might be good for someone, but definitely not for you. Therefore it is a vice.

If you try to help someone without them asking, it feels like an invasion for the person you are trying to impose help on. Nothing good will come out of it. It is also a vice when you disrespect someone's choice. Like me trying to help a homeless person find a job when he only wanted money.

With ITT, we will replace the beliefs with virtues that help you. These will be downloaded instantly and without any unpleasant effects.

How Instant Transformation Technique works

To get into brain frequency of your choice (neither is better or worse, it's just a matter of preference), I will talk you through the process. You can perform this without me once you know and can remember the full process. But for now, I have made available a completely free ITT recording, which you can download from my website at www.prosperitycode.co.uk.

Once you have downloaded the recording, I would like you to find a quiet spot, press play, and follow the instructions. During the process, I will help you achieve different frequencies.

I will then guide you through a series of questions designed to help unblock your beliefs and self-limiting patterns.

Of course, this process is much quicker and more effective working 1-2-1 with a qualified practitioner. However, you'll be surprised by how quickly this starts to work compared with other modalities you may have used.

Method for Change – Simple, Easy and Fun

I have been to hundreds of seminars, meditations, lessons, spiritual practices, and the methods I discovered were either too complex or not very clear, or required a special skill like clairvoyance or clairaudience, or physical strength.

I asked for simpler ways to transform my life, and I received the answers. And I want to share this system with you, so you can have the life that you want, and you can make any changes you want.

Some people say: If you can't do anything about the situation, change your attitude to it.

It is untrue: you can change both or either change the situation or change your attitude to it. What is a better way? And, also, what is the cause and what is the effect?

Some believe that what's inside is more important than outside. I say: what's inside, the same is outside, there is no inside or outside, it is inseparable.

Whatever your life is right now, it is a manifestation, reflection, or direct consequence of your inner world: beliefs, thoughts, wishes, desires. In order to change the outside, you need to change your inside and learn to accept it.

There are millions of ways to do the same job and achieve

the same result or similar quality of outcome, because of the law of abundance and creativity. The most important question is: what is the most pleasant, quickest, and fun way (or whichever description you like to choose for yourself) to achieve what you want?

Questions here are all-important because whatever you are going to ask, you are going to get the answer to.

From doing many transformation sessions and in conversations with God, I realised that our soul and higher-self design our life with love and ingenuity as an amazing adventure and a game. It feels exciting to play in this body on this planet. We have a divine plan to reach our highest potential. If we remember to stay in the flow with love, joy, excitement, acceptance, and full awareness, our path is going to be enjoyable, fun, and easy.

If we start resisting, rejecting some bits, and pick and choose what to accept, we get stuck in a particular situation, and we don't move on to other bits of our divine plan. If we created a block and we are not on schedule, we can't move on to the next amazing adventure, so our mind tries to fill the time with something. But the more negative and angry you are, the worse scenarios you create, instead of your highest potential.

Just to give you an example of what I mean, here is a story:

Say a very dear person to a someone has left, and they don't accept the situation. They keep crying, grieving, get angry at the person, who left, themselves, God, whoever they choose.

Things start getting worse and worse the longer they are stuck in that scenario. Stage one could be that they sit and wait for their dear person to return. They don't move on; they don't want to talk or see other people, and they don't go to work because they are afraid to miss them.

Stage 2 could be getting worse, when they get depressed over it, get into financial troubles, and things start snowballing.

At Stage 3, a person can get so stressed out that they get very sick or even die.

What the intended scenario was supposed to be in that

person's life plan: to learn to accept things for what they are, the fact of what happened, to live with awareness and acceptance of the other person's choice and free will, with trust and faith, that whatever happened was for the better and greater good of all parties. You realise you have a choice to either sit and cry or you can go out and play because nobody is responsible for your choices, feelings, and emotions apart from you. You know the world is abundant and you can find a way to entertain yourself and make yourself feel happy again. As soon as you are in the flow again, miracles start happening.

Life is full of gifts and surprises. You follow your divine plan and meet the love of your life, a new opportunity for your career, a new hobby or something else to change your life and make it even more amazing. So what do you hold in store for yourself? What areas of life do you try to control and don't allow yourself to enjoy life the most? What opportunities or situations don't you allow to happen, that can benefit you in every way?

The Energy Substitute Method

Don't overthink. There is no right or wrong, just follow your internal feelings, emotions, or intuition. Close your eyes or keep them open, whatever you prefer.

If you think you can't visualise, believe me, you can. Can you think of a lemon? Do you know what it looks or tastes like? Sure, you can, and you do.

Think of an issue you want to resolve. Say, you want to double your income, but you don't know how and where to turn or where to look to resolve the issue.

Here's what to do:

1. Think of an issue.
2. Think of what you want/your goal/your wish.

3. Focus on your feelings and emotions and listen to yourself.

4. Identify emotions that don't serve you or stop you from getting what you want (like fear, lack of knowledge, shyness, doubt).

5. Imagine/feel/see/smell/taste or hear yourself (whatever your leading sense is) as a mirror image or a shape and see, hear, or feel, a particular energy that you identified (say, doubt in yourself). You can also imagine it in colour, sound, smell, or touch.

6. Now ask unconditional love (Energy of Creation of All That Is) to transform doubt into unconditional love, and witness doubt in you transform into white light.

7. Add any resources that you want or are lacking, such as confidence, faith, power, strength, etc. Ask unconditional love to add faith and imagine it as a ray of coloured light being added to the image of you (notice what colour it is). You can also witness it as a feeling, sound, smell, or taste.

8. Do you feel different? If not quite there yet, ask yourself again, what quality you dislike about yourself – say, self-criticism. Repeat the process and feel if the issue has been resolved.

9. Repeat until you feel the difference in a pleasant way for you.

Let Energy of Creation do the Work Method

1. State the request– say you want to heal eyesight or financial situation, whatever it might be.

2. Request: Unconditional Love (or God, or Energy of Creation, or Creator of All That Is), please uncreate, delete, and remove all the beliefs that caused this issue and download all the lacking or missing virtues (resources) or skills.

3. State how you want it done – please do it in the quickest, efficient, comfortable, and pleasant for me, way. Thank you, please show me.
4. Witness the process in colours, sounds, feelings, smells, or taste (whichever you prefer). What goes in; what comes out?
5. Continue until you feel lighter or happier, so it is a noticeable change. Sometimes you can get distracted and float away in your thoughts; if that happens, just repeat the request and keep witnessing it.

On the seminars and webinars I teach in more detail how to apply my methods. It does not have to be only in Theta state, although you might feel more intuitive in it. You can do it in Beta, Gamma, or Alpha also. I don't have a belief that Theta state is better than Beta or Alpha anymore (thanks to one of my students Katia, who pointed it out). I learnt so much from my wonderful students, too.

Everything you ever wanted ... just ASK!

As you'll see from my story so far, I've learnt a lot, and I've not made any mistakes. But that's impossible, you might say! What I also understood is: there is no such thing as a mistake in the highest truth of The Creator!

There is just an experience pleasant or unpleasant. You either learn to do something well from experience, or you learn it by direct knowledge by asking your intuition, whether a particular experience would be beneficial for you. That knowledge you just trust. You don't need to stick your fingers in a socket to know it will not be pleasant. The same with everything. You just know what will be good for you and what will not. If you want to cause yourself trouble anyway, who am I to stop you?!

Whenever we get advice from someone, go to seminars or learn from books, all we are doing is learning about someone else's experience and receive information.

I want to be clear on this so you really 'get' it. It's an important distinction.

When we learn about someone's opinion or their experience, it is not true knowledge. It's just their experience or opinion.

You can only receive true knowledge from The Creator.

Sure, you can ask The Creator whether the knowledge or advice you have been given is true and correct. Everyone sees the truth through the prism of their belief system, so it might not be the whole story.

Everything in this book is my experience. I'm sharing my story with you. It's up to you to decide how you can use it to help you achieve what you want (or just ask The Creator!).

The importance of the question

Before we continue, let's just talk about the importance of questions because you're going to be asking a lot of them very soon!

If you ask questions, you always get the answers, so make sure you ask the right ones.

For example, instead of asking: "Why am I so silly to keep getting in trouble?" ask: "How can I fix this?" or "How can I be wiser?"

Do you notice the difference?

From doing multiple sessions with instructors of Theta healing or Reiki, I found that some people have a major issue they keep working on. It could be illnesses, money or relationship challenges. Working on different illnesses seems to be a perpetual job. Once one thing is healed, another illness comes up.

Healing is a process, and health is a state, so the question is, do you want to be healthy, or do you want to participate in continuous healings? Why ask for healing of a particular illness, if you can fix all health issues in one go?

If you figure out what the benefits are of being ill or

unhealthy and lessons to be learnt, maybe you will not need to be unhealthy anymore. You might say: but how can I possibly benefit from being sick?

Well, think about situations when you had lots of work and deadlines, and you wouldn't allow yourself to slow down or rest. You kept pushing and pushing yourself until you collapsed with a cold or migraine.

In this situation, you did not give yourself permission to rest or relax, so your body forced you to rest. The lesson is to love and respect your body, rest and relax when you are tired. Once you do that, you will not need to get ill in order to rest.

Another reason could be not getting enough love or attention from family and friends, so when people get sick, everyone tries to find time to visit. Why not learn to spend more time with your loved ones because you all want to be together and not because someone is sick or dying?

I always treated my kids the same healthy or ill, so they learnt that they would not get more attention by being sick. That way, they prefer to be healthy. There could be other reasons why people choose to be sick, so remember to remove all the benefits of lack of health and choose to have perfect health. The same process will apply to all the other issues in life like lack of money or relationships issues.

How to do this yourself (use your human intuition)

I know what you're probably thinking, right now.

"This is all fine and good, Tania, but how do I tap into this when I don't have a good intuition or how do I know if my intuition is any good?"

First, know that you can do this! As I'm about to show you, you have all the intuitive senses available. The reason you don't know it yet, is you don't use them enough. We've been taught to ignore intuition and rely on logic or rational thinking.

Second, know that you can develop these, either by yourself

or with a teacher. Through my seminars and workshops, I show students how to reconnect with their intuition. You already have it and use it, to some extent.

I've already shown you how the brain works and how it operates on different frequencies, with each frequency allowing you to access different abilities. We can be working using different states. I am used to working in Theta state, but it can be any other.

Before we do that, we need to understand better your own intuitive abilities and powers.

Picture the scene. It's a drinks reception, and you're holding a glass of wine and chatting to others standing around you. The host walks up to your group with a gentleman beside him and introduces him to you.

He looks you in the eye, says "Hello" with a smile, and shakes your hand.

If you were in this situation, what could you immediately know about him?

If you talk to someone, can you pretty much tell if they like you or if they hate you? Yes.

If you look at someone, can you pretty much tell if they are lying or if they are telling the truth? Yes.

And if you've just met someone, can you tell if they are successful or pretending to be, or just a beginner?

It's very obvious, isn't it? In some cases, it is more obvious, but you can always tell these things.

Intuition is the ability to understand something from a feeling or instinctive knowledge, rather than understand it from logical reasoning.

As soon as you enter a room full of people, you read everyone instantly. You know everything there is to know about every person there. You just don't bring it onto a conscious level.

The gifts you are born with

When you tap into your intuition, you bring to the conscious level the gifts you already have. Let's explore these. We all have senses like eyesight, hearing, touch, taste, and smell. We also have these duplicated on an intuitive level.

Clairvoyance

For eyesight, we have clairvoyance and the 'third eye'. Your clairvoyant abilities allow you to see things that are not perceived by your normal, everyday senses. For example, highly developed clairvoyants can read thoughts or obtain accurate body scans or future readings.

Clairaudience

For hearing, we have clairaudience and the ability to hear what is inaudible to our normal hearing. Sometimes, it can be felt as words of warning or directing you to a course of action to protect you, as if it was from a Guardian Angel or The Creator. Messages can also come from dark spirits, and it is important to have clarity about who you are listening to and who is talking.

Clairsentience

For thinking, we have clairsentience – or clairknowing (my own term) – which is knowing things that would otherwise remain hidden or getting answers to your questions as a clear thought.

Taste and Smell also exist on an intuitive level.

If I ask you: can you smell the truth or lies? Most likely, the majority of people will not even question the expression and will understand the meaning of it.

Empathy

For feeling, we have empathy. Empathy, in this sense, goes beyond our everyday understanding of the word and allows us to feel what others feel.

Now that last one is an intuitive sense that is widely recognised among people. Maybe you're highly empathetic yourself or know someone who is so well-tuned into others' feelings.

We don't question empathy. However, some people are much more sceptical of the other intuitive senses and, as a result, stop listening to them and taking action, because they don't trust them.

In case you wondered, you already have all of these. You are clairvoyant. You are clairsentient. You are clairaudient. The question is not whether you are or not. You are. Most definitely.

The question is how well or often you tap into and listen to these.

Your intuition is the tool to help you make better decisions and listen to what you know is right in your heart. Master this, and you will discover a whole new world you did not notice before.

If you would like to learn how to develop your intuitive senses further in-person, go to www.prosperitycode.co.uk to discover when my next workshop is running.

How to get rich and not die trying

*"I don't want to make money.
I just want to be wonderful."*

MARILYN MONROE

Ways to make more money

In this section of the book, I'm going to show you how to create an abundant future and make money doing what you love.

You've done the hard work of identifying and removing the beliefs and blocks that don't serve you. You have replaced those beliefs with strong virtues that will help and serve you in a helpful and loving way instead of destruction. With these in place, you have the foundation for transforming your income and wealth situation.

(OK, serious teacher face on now. If you skipped the exercises at the start of this book and came straight back here to find out juicy wealth tips, stop! This isn't going to work unless you've worked on releasing your restrictive beliefs first. I'm not joking! Go back and do them now. Yes, right now!)

I will show you the equation to making your first million (and your next million and so on) and widen your horizons about how you can make money. We'll brainstorm some ideas together.

For most people reading this, building a business will be the fastest, easiest way to turn your hobby into something that makes you lots of money.

I know how to build a successful business. I've done it.

But it's possible to get it wrong, like many businesses that fail every year. This is why so many people fear to start a business. But think about it this way: if you start a business with little or no money and learn many new skills on the way, meet interesting people, try some new cool things, if it fails down the line, you still have your knowledge, fun experiences, stories to tell (like I have done in this book) and your new contacts instead of a perceived risk. That's why it's important I show you the strategies to turn your passion into profit.

And you're going to be learning a few lessons from the best in the world.

You see, very early on, I knew how important it was to get the right coaching from the very best mentors and experts in the world.

I paid Jay Abraham $25,000 for phone call sessions on business and marketing advice. I learned from the master of sales, inspiration, and speaking, Brian Tracy. We shared the stage with and have spoken to Robert Kiyosaki on a few occasions.

I met Richard Branson at the launch of Virgin Galactic. At the end of the presentation, we got talking about wealth creation and business strategies. I started my education listening to these guys. I now include myself in the list of financial experts, as I consider myself qualified enough to talk about money.

On the *Money Magic* course, we go into detail on all the important lessons these wealth gurus taught me. While I don't cover all the lessons in this book, I'll share with you the most important principles I've learned from these gurus on:

- Setting your business vision
- Valuing your time

- Building a team
- Following your passion
- Finding resources
- Publicising your business
- And much more

We'll start by focusing on how to manifest the success you really want. And it all comes down to thinking about lemons …

Want to learn all the wealth secrets of these gurus? Join the *Money Magic* workshop to go deep on wealth advice and strategies from Richard Branson, Robert Kiyosaki, Jay Abraham, and Brian Tracy. For more details go to www.prosperitycode.co.uk.

Stop making decisions you regret (and live free of fear)

When we are inspired, and we make decisions from a loving and resourceful state, then we always make the right decisions.

But then fear kicks in, and people worry … "Oh, what have I done?" And they panic. They experience buyer's remorse or even at the moment of handing over money or on the verge of doing something good or great they think, "Oh, it's going to cause me so much stress and so much pressure."

Fear is a low vibrational frequency. When we function in that kind of state, we always make the wrong decisions. Instead of expanding our abundance, we start restricting it.

How do we stay out of fears and doubts and spend more of our time feeling generous, kind, worthy, and loved? How do we feel inspired and happy all the time? How do we make the right decisions?

Our thoughts are material. What we think has the power to create our reality. If your thoughts are pure and positive, you will manage to create what you want faster. If your thoughts are pessimistic, angry, or jealous, the opposite happens.

Don't believe your thoughts create your reality? Here's another test for you …

Picture a lemon, change your reality

Think of a lemon. Like this one ...

Imagine this very sour lemon in your mouth. It's *very, very* sour.

Now hold that picture in your mind – you may even want to close your eyes for a few moments to picture that sour lemon.

What happens? You start salivating.

How could you *possibly* start salivating when there is no lemon there ...

... just the thought of a lemon in your mind?

The cool thing about the brain is this – it doesn't know the difference between the reality and the imagined. We can hold an image of something in our minds, and it will produce a physical effect. It's the same with thoughts of fears.

Just think about the implications this has ...

And use this ability to your advantage by imagining how you want your life to be and what you want to have. The more you focus on it and the more feeling and emotion you bring into the picture, the more likely it will materialise in your life.

What do you want to be, do or have?

I'm going to get science-y again, briefly.

Our brain has a wave-collapsing function. We know this from physics at school.

If you remember the popular experiment when scientists bombard a screen with photons – particles of light – and depending on whether someone witnessed the experiment or not, light either behaved as a particle or it behaved like a wave.

It means the photon could appear randomly in different times and places simultaneously.

When we watch, the world freezes into the reality we know.

When we're not watching, it's a quantum soup of billions of possibilities.

The question is, given a choice, how would you freeze your reality? You can do it any way you want.

Like this …

Or this …

Or this ...

... or WHATEVER you desire?

(If you don't believe this is true or you've not heard about this experiment, go Google it. Be prepared to be left dumbstruck!)

Our thoughts create reality

Are you starting to understand now what I meant when I wrote earlier that you have the power to recreate your life?

We can use the power of the mind and thoughts for manifesting our goals and our desired lifestyle.

If you imagine enough times what you want, engaging all your senses and feelings, your brain recreates what you want in your reality.

Isn't that cool?

I think it's pretty amazing and powerful, too. Your thoughts are material, which means you have the power to create material changes.

Microbiologist Bruce Lipton highlights the power of positive thinking in his research by advocating the idea that you can reprogram your subconscious to change your genetic code and many processes in your body.

He suggests that your genes don't cause disease, your beliefs do. I actually consider poverty a disease. "Your beliefs, thoughts, and feelings can change any process in the body on a genetic or molecular level."

If you can change your body on a genetic or molecular level, you can change any aspect of your life with the power of thought and The Creator's help.

How making money is easy, simple and fun when you play The Game

Have you heard the claim that 1% of the population controls 99% of all the wealth in the world?

This 1% controls all the money and all the resources. This elite does everything it can to protect its wealth and stop others breaking into the circle.

It's why people believe: "Other people are in this global elite, and I'm not. That's why I'm not rich."

There's one problem: it's false!

This is a collective belief. Behind it is the belief that resources are limited. Thinking this way also puts responsibilities on someone else for your finances and abundance. Making money is easy, simple, and fun. Some have lost sight of it.

The truth is we're all equal.

The virtue of equanimity means we are all the same for The Creator of All That Is. God loves us all equally. Everyone is worthy of unlimited abundance of the universe if they wish to have it and are ready to accept it.

There's a warning.

Whatever you ask from The Creator will come to you instantly and unconditionally, if you can accept it. You need to be aware that it can come into your life in a different way than you were expecting.

That's why it's important for us to have gratitude and be open-minded. If something comes your way, and it's not how you expected it to be, you may not be able to accept it. You may feel disappointed. This won't help your wealth or your abundance.

Playing The Game is about fun, enjoyment, and happiness. Some people make The Game more 'interesting' by creating barriers, obstacles, and difficulties, therefore restricting their abundance.

Some people have lost the memory of who they truly are. Every person is divine by nature. You don't have to be hard on yourself and make it difficult.

The way to do this is to focus on how to create your abundance easily from doing something you actually love.

You don't have to struggle to succeed

It's strongly in some of our genetics that everything must be a struggle.

Our ancestors tried to survive and they had to struggle in life. My ancestors went through at least three wars – the First, Civil and Second World War – and maybe some of your family members did, too. They encountered shortages of food and periods of starvation that threatened their lives. They were deficient in pretty much everything – shelter, clothes, and rest. Our genetics carry the memory of that suffering.

They believed life is a fight. It's very much irrelevant for our times, but it is a powerful underlying problem.

I am rich, and I'm abundant now, and I worked with it a lot.

If you want to create abundance, you need a particular set of virtues when it comes to building wealth:

- Flexibility
- Respect
- Responsibility
- Communication
- Interaction
- Eloquence
- Passion
- Acceptance
- Abundance
- Creativity
- And many more

You can pick and choose from whom you want to learn and what you want to learn. Instead of reinventing the wheel, take the wheel that already exists and improve on it. There is no need to reinvent something that is already there.

There is an abundance of absolutely everything in the universe. In the truth of The Creator, you cannot really come up with something drastically new. When it comes down to it, everything is a combination of somebody else's ideas already in existence.

According to statistics, a new millionaire is created every 60 seconds.

Think about it. Every 60 seconds someone, somewhere becomes a millionaire. So make sure it's YOU!

Sixty seconds and BOOM, you're a millionaire. Isn't it wonderful?

What do you need to create that million?

Never before in the history of humanity have there been so many opportunities before us. We have great resources, such as the internet. You can set up a business and serve customers all over the world.

And the cool thing is, it can be even easier if you follow someone else's path. I've had times in my life when I worked 20-hour days, seven days a week. It wasn't easy, but it was worth it. It doesn't have to be difficult for you if you follow some of my recommendations in the next few pages. If you invest a lot into 15% of the process of your business, then 85% of it will come much easier.

Choose your vision

"Why fit in, when you were born to stand out?"

DR SEUSS

Everything you do will fail without this

How do you know what to do, if you don't know what you want?

Being rich or wealthy may be one of your goals but ask yourself – why?

Why do I want to have money?

What do I really want?

What is your true motivation?

Having a clear goal isn't just important for you. If you have a mission or a business that needs the support of others, you need to know your vision, so you can sell it to the right people and take them with you. If you have a team, you need to be able to show them exactly what you're trying to achieve.

If everyone is clear and shares your vision, you can move everyone in the same direction together.

If you have people pulling in different directions, that's not going to be very helpful. You need to make sure you have a vision for your business for the next three, five and ten years.

Right now, you may think, "Oh my God in ten years I can achieve absolutely everything!" That is very true. But to achieve anything, you should at least know what you actually want and have it as a clear and measurable goal.

Exercise – What's my vision?

Let's work out what you actually want to achieve. First, let's look at your beliefs (you should be really good at this question now!).

What are your beliefs about money, about running a business, or about selling your services, your time or the goods you produce? Do you believe running a business is risky or hard? Does it take all of your time or can you do it easily, effortlessly, and quickly? Do you need a team? What kind of team, and how many people? Do you believe you can start a business with no money, or you must have capital?

Now, take some time to reflect and think on these questions:

What is the purpose of the business, and where are you going?

What do you want to achieve in one year?

Five years?

Ten years?

Always have a clear mission. By mission, I mean what is your actual goal and your target in your business? Do you want to have a worldwide brand? Do you want to be the biggest in your country or your city? Or maybe just the biggest in your area?

Not everyone will even want to build a large business. You may be content with a one-person business because it fits with your lifestyle and could be easier, or it doesn't require as many resources.

If you're not sure, then the best question to ask is: what do you want your life to look like? Lots of travel and time off to do what you want? Or winning lots of business awards and meeting people? Picture exactly what that looks like. Manifest your reality.

Understanding how you want your life to look in one, five, and ten years' time will help you work out what your business needs to look like if you want a balanced life while running a business or making money.

Once you have a clear vision and goals, the next thing is to work out what steps you need to take and what actions to take daily to achieve that vision.

Why you should leverage your time

"Why do you need a housekeeper to clean the whole seven square metres of your room?!"

My friends couldn't understand it. Like them, I didn't have much money. I had a small apartment to myself. But now they were questioning why I was spending money on a cleaner … for a small studio.

Everything in life needs to be balanced. Your business, family life, your hobbies, and other activities. That's really important, and in order for you to get some free time, you need to learn to delegate. I learnt that when I was 21, that's when I hired my first helper for £5 an hour.

I realised my time was worth £100 per hour back then, so for every hour the cleaner cleaned and did house chores while I worked, I made a profit of £95. That was my way of thinking. If I could focus 16 hours a day on what I liked doing while growing my business instead of cleaning, I made a profit by hiring help for unqualified jobs.

That's why I hired a cleaner at 21.

Creating abundance is not a goal of life. It's a given. And we either accept it into our life or not. Money is not a goal, either. It's a side effect of you doing something you love and producing value or means to get what you want. Being happy while doing that is true success.

I'm going to show you how to win back hours of your time each week while hitting every goal you ever set. You're going to love this.

(You can thank me for this, any time ... :))

Let's start with something called The 80/20 Rule. This rule claims only a small proportion of your activity is responsible for the majority of the results you get.

For example, 20% of your customers generate 80% of your income. Or 20% of your products make up 80% of sales. This applies to all aspects. Time, effort, and personal life.

So 20% of your hobbies take up 80% of your time. Or 20% of the food in your kitchen makes up 80% of your meals. It's everywhere.

These days, it is more like 90:10.

But here's the amazing part that will change your life.

Understand that 90% of the most productive things you do in your day or your week take up only 10% of your time.

Let that sink in.

For all the hours you have in a week, 10% of your time produces 90% of the results you get from that.

So what about the rest of the time? It's wasted or spent doing things that aren't productive.

Go on, be honest with yourself. It's true, isn't it?

If you want to change your life, work out what the 10% of things you do are the most productive, and cut out everything else or make them productive for something else.

We all have the same amount of time available. Whether it's you, me, or Richard Branson or Warren Buffett, we only have 24 hours in a day.

The difference is that those who succeed, know how to use those hours best.

The 'secret' is to act in harmony with yourself and your goals. What you spend most of your time thinking and doing produces the relevant result.

If you want to make £1 million in business or from trading, are you focusing on the relevant thoughts and actions? Or do you complain about how you never have time for it?

Or is most of your time spent going to the gym or playing football?

There's nothing wrong with going to the gym or playing football.

If your goal is to be fit and healthy, you would be on the right track.

But, if your goal is £1 million, then your actions are out of alignment with your goals.

Admit it to yourself. Right now, do you feel like what you do day after day is in line with what you really want?

That's why it's essential to be clear on your goals and also be clear on where you spend your time.

Think how you can balance your actions each day, so you're in harmony with your goals.

You always need to think about how you can maximise the time you have.

This next exercise will help you do that.

Exercise – Time-goal alignment

Take a blank piece of paper and draw a line down the middle of it.

On the left-hand side, make a list of all your actions over the next 24–48 hours.

Write down everything you do and how long you spent doing it. Don't overthink it – get everything written down in the left-hand column. If you're super-busy, use more sheets of paper if necessary.

This is the first part of the exercise.

Once you've completed this, turn over the page for the next part.

Now, on your piece of paper, you should have a left-hand column filled with your actions during the day.

In the right-hand column, I want you to write down your goals.

What is it you want to achieve in every area of your life?

Or do?

Or be?

It could be 'earn £1 million'. It could be 'be a great parent' or 'be a great friend'. Whatever these are, write them down.

Now go back through your actions on the left-hand side. Identify whether each action you took helped to achieve any of the goals in the right-hand column.

Big, important statement coming up ...

THIS WILL CHANGE YOUR LIFE!

When you analyse how you spend your day against what your goals are, you see the reality.

Most of us don't act in alignment with what we want.

But that's great news because now you KNOW. All you need to do to reach your goals faster is choose to stop doing what doesn't help you and do more of what does.

Identify the 10% that's productive. Cut out what isn't. Do more of what is effective and useful in the time you save by deleting activities that don't help you. And make sure you enjoy all that! If you think you have to force yourself to do something you hate to get closer to your goal, it is the wrong action or path you chose. Be creative and think of something that you love doing, and it will be serving you in achieving goals.

Think about this in terms of the Urgent vs Important Matrix, seen here:

URGENT VS IMPORTANT

	URGENT.	NOT URGENT
IMPORTANT	**Crisis** **deadlines** **problems**	**Opportunities** **Planning** **relationships**
NOT IMPORTANT	**Calls** **Emails** **Meetings** **interruptions**	**Busy work** **Time wastes** **Random calls** **emails**

As you can see, there are four different types of work. If you don't value your time effectively, you can easily end up spending a lot of time working in the first quadrant – Urgent and Important. That's a bad place to be. If you're getting too many things into the quadrant, it means you have neglected that area and left things too late. While other people will tell you to double your focus on trying to keep out of there, I look at this differently. Whose deadlines are you working to that are so urgent? Yours? Or someone else's?

Also, do you actually need to do this or want to do it? If the answer is no, stop it. When you become aware of this, you learn to say no to things you hate and say yes to things you like and bring you joy. When you love doing what you're doing, it's easy to stay out of the first Quadrant.

Use this in all areas of your life.

Then ask yourself:

What should I start doing?

What should I stop doing?

What puts me more in alignment with my goals?

This will change how you value your time

How valuable do you feel your time is? How valuable do you feel your skills are? If you're employed, how much does your boss value you? Or, if you have your own business, how much do your clients value you?

Try to be as honest as possible with yourself. Are they prepared to pay for your time, and are you prepared to accept money for it? That is another question.

You should get paid what you're worth. If you invest time and money learning a skill or becoming an expert that helps others, you deserve to get paid well.

Sometimes people worry about how much they charge or don't want to charge a lot because they think others will believe it to be too expensive. If you provide value to your customers, and they get the result they want, that is your value. It has nothing to do with others' lack of money.

The other side of valuing time is not wasting it doing things, which don't serve or help you.

For a start, don't waste time on useless things that don't give you pleasure. Don't blankly stare at the TV watching programmes that don't interest you that much or read a book you don't enjoy. (How often have you started a book and found it difficult to give up until you finished, even though it was not interesting for you?)

Likewise, don't sit in a boring conference or meeting or talk to people that you don't enjoy spending time with.

It's your choice. Your time is precious, too precious to waste in a boring meeting. Seriously, get up and walk out of there!

Learn to respect your time and time of other people. Each interaction should bring you joy or purpose. If you catch yourself feeling bored, either find something fun in that interaction ... or get rid of it.

Why you can't cost-cut your way to great wealth

Contrary to the current accepted wisdom of finding ways to cut costs in your life, I'm a believer in paying as much as possible to get the best.

Seriously! Like the previous example with the law firm, it pays to pay the best.

Saving, scrimping, and cost-cutting are contrary to an abundant mindset. And, more importantly, it will make you unhappy.

"Cut out your morning latte ... "

"Buy cheaper brand food ... "

"Check every label until you've got the cheapest, lowest-ever deal ... "

This is the kind of sad advice given by personal finance 'gurus' to encourage you to stop spending money on what makes you happy and instead squeeze those moments of joy from your day.

I disagree. Completely and totally.

Here's why. Many years ago, I purchased a week's worth of coaching from legendary marketing coach, Jay Abraham. As a bit of background, Jay is a guy who has been responsible for over $20 billion of sales in his career and is the world's highest-paid marketing consultant.

The cost for a week of training with Jay was $25,000.

(Right there is a good test of your money beliefs – how did you feel when you saw his price tag?)

To me, it was a bargain. To have Jay brainstorm about my business for a whole week and bring his 40 years of experience in building and growing businesses to the value of many, many millions *only* cost me $25,000.

In that week, I learned so much from him that would have taken me years to discover for myself. That $25,000 saved me time ... the only commodity money can't buy.

It was during one session that he made his most profound comment that has stuck with me to this day. It proves everything I've been saying to this point. The best advice he gave me was:

"You cannot cost-cut your way to success."

No matter how many expenses you get rid of, you will never get rich through cutting costs. You need to improve your thinking. You need to think big, expand your business, and grow your cash flow, your sales, and your revenue. Success is not about cutting costs.

Why paying the most pays off the most

When we started, we made an incredibly sensible decision: we hired the most expensive and knowledgeable people to assist our team.

Big firms deal with huge projects and major mergers and acquisitions, and we were just two girls doing not much of anything. However, we wanted to have the best companies backing us in case anything went wrong.

This is how we picked our lawyers and accountants. We called all the City firms and asked how much they charged per hour.

If the lawyer said £300 per hour, we thought, "Okay, too cheap – they're unsuitable."

Then the next would quote £500 per hour; we thought, "Okay, but pass."

Eventually, we spoke to one firm who quoted us £1500 per hour. We thought, "Okay, that's the one," – so we signed up with them.

Very quickly, we saw the benefit of working with the best.

The very first thing they did was get us a VAT exemption. With just one phone call, they found a loophole that allowed us to be classified as an educational business – which, of course, we were. It cost us a reasonably small amount of money at the time – around £5000 – but that VAT exemption saved us hundreds of thousands of pounds in the future.

Finding the most expensive adviser or expert actually managed to save us a significant amount of money. On a million-pound revenue with VAT at 18% (at the time), well … you can do the maths. That's how much they saved us per year for the rest of our life.

It worked well for them, too. Every time I started a new business, I ran right back to the same law firm and hired them to do the same thing again.

How to ignore the critics and get stuff done

Brian Tracy says that some things don't need to be perfect; they just need to get done. It doesn't matter if you can do them better or not; it's completely irrelevant. There are specific actions in a business that just need to be done without thinking too much.

So, if you haven't started the business, and you're delaying because you haven't chosen the best vehicle for tax efficiency or whether it should be a limited company or LLP or something else, the point is just to get started. You can always redo the company and make changes later. The important thing is to get on with doing those things without delays and excuses.

If you're in that situation, think why you're stalling and what is the true reason behind it. Why are you sabotaging your progress? Sometimes we need to do something like action in its purest form that doesn't require thought. It just requires attention to get it done and, boom, it's done.

And, by the way, there is no such thing as a mistake.

One belief that slows people down and leads them to delay action due to perfectionism is they don't want to be judged for their mistakes. But there isn't such a thing as a mistake, only an experience from which you can learn.

Thomas Edison, inventor of the lightbulb, took 1000 attempts to invent the lightbulb. When asked how he felt about failing 999 times, he said he did not fail 999 times. He simply discovered 999 ways not to make a light bulb. There are no mistakes, just a learning curve.

Here's the point. The same people who criticise you are the same people who just do nothing and sit and watch television and produce zero value for themselves and others.

Are you a winner or a whiner?

You will ruin your life if you're a serial complainer, cynic, or a critic. You may not even realise it.

The best way to discover if you are is to look at your mindset.

When faced with a goal, do you think, "Yes, I can," and "Why not?"

When you encounter a problem, do you think: "What an opportunity!" and "Let's get started!"?

Do you jump out of bed in the morning ready to enjoy the day?

If you answered "YES!" to all these, you have the mindset of a winner.

That's exactly what you need to succeed in life, business, investing, trading, and making money.

But, remember, there are serial achievers and the complete opposite:

The constant whiner and moaner.

Make sure this person is not you. They're an expert at finding excuses for why they've not got what they wanted. They encounter problems, and their first instinct is to complain or give up. They're desperate to find someone to blame. They shake off all responsibility for their actions.

You either know someone who fits the mould ... or you may recognise yourself as this perpetual moaner: no time, weather is bad, the economic climate is wrong, the family is against you or the whole world.

Many people who get into business find that it doesn't always work out the first time. They may have attracted the wrong partners or worked with incompatible customers.

A person with a complainer's mindset won't take responsibility. They will trot out the excuse: they can't trust people anymore. Or they're fearful of getting 'ripped off' again. But they don't understand that they attracted these people and situations.

Someone with a winning mindset will act differently and think differently. A winner will acknowledge that whatever happened was their responsibility. It was their choice to attract the wrong partners and customers. Importantly, they will see this situation as an opportunity to do better again in the future. They learn from each experience.

Complainers never learn anything because they never believe it was their own creation.

Think about it this way: if a dog bites you once, it may be a fluke. But if five other dogs bite you again, it's a pattern.

Maybe – just maybe – the problem is you.

There is a reason why you attract these situations into your life. The problem is that people can be unaware of why things happen a certain way. And that's why I want you to start being mindful of this.

Over the next 24 hours, pay attention to how you react when something happens. Do you complain or do you step up? Seriously, this is enlightening. Once you know, you can identify and remove the underlying beliefs causing you to complain. When you remove the beliefs that sabotage your success, you stop attracting negative people or situations.

Unlimited ways to make money

"Do what you love and the money will follow"

MARSHA SINETAR

When it comes to thinking about how you can make money, you hear so much scarcity in the language of some people.

How often have you heard people complain that everything has already been invented or launched or that another company 'stole' their idea? (Sure, you had that idea in your head for ten years and did nothing with it!)

There is and always will be abundance. There will always be plenty of ways to make money. You just need to be open to finding them.

When you come from a place of infinity, you'll never be short of an endless stream of ideas. And I should know because I'm continually coming up with hundreds of business ideas. (Seriously, jump on a call with me, and I fire out ideas like a machine gun!)

You probably know one or two ways to make money outside having a job – maybe property, stocks and shares, investing and so on. How about I show you at least another 20 ways of creating money you probably hadn't even thought of?

Anyway, let's test that right now …

Exercise – More than one way to make money

For this exercise, I want you to come up with additional ways of getting money.

Now, most people earn money from a job, and you may have a job right now, so income from employment is one of the channels of receiving money.

You probably also know that you can make money from investing, and so that's a second way. But I would like you to come up with as many ways as you can think of, to bring more money into your life.

(There's at least 20 ways I believe you can reel off the top of your head right away – but, of course, there are many, many more.)

Do this now before you move on.

OK, so you should have come up with a whole list which included ideas such as:

- Selling old items
- Manifesting money
- Having a business
- Selling ideas
- Inheritance
- Providing a service
- Receiving money as a gift
- Investing
- Winning the lottery
- Bounty and treasure hunting
- Finding money

The list could go on and on. What this is really designed to do is show you there are so many ways for money and wealth to come into your life.

When you have a very developed version of acceptance, you can simply decide that you can now start accepting money from everyone and everything, no matter which way and from where it comes.

I used business and then investing to create multiple streams of income with a diversified portfolio, so whatever happened with the economy of a particular country, I would be fine. I am writing this during the coronavirus pandemic when most people cannot go to work or have income. It has never been busier and more profitable for me. When some streams of income stop, others, like stock market trading, are massively generous with profits. Over the years of working on myself, I have developed strong faith and confidence in myself: no matter what happens, I am always fine. And money-wise, it just appears, when I want it … even though I could have been a billionaire TWICE over, and I have not become one just yet …

How I failed to become a billionaire. Twice.

Here's a tale of how I left behind something that wasn't my true passion … and forfeited the chance to become a billionaire. Twice. With NO regrets!

The first time was with a property opportunity. I was looking for an office in 2006 and found two more or less suitable spaces in London around Tower Bridge and London Bridge. One was 360 m2 priced around £800,000 and another was 5000 m2, priced at £5 million.

The first one had a nice normal office space with a large enough hall to make a conference room out of it. The second was a two-storey building with a college/educational grading. I was focused on finding an office space, and the 360 m2 space was plenty for that purpose. I did consider the other option but thought that trying to rent out extra space would be too much hassle.

The developers had other views, so they acquired it, and now it has become a lovely development – Tower Hill 1 – now worth at least a billion pounds.

I got what I wanted, and so did they. Everyone got exactly what they were looking for. I did not see the full potential because my focus was elsewhere.

Next time, I had an idea to go big and start an internet business for copy trading, similar to eToro. It seemed like a logical and complementary match to my existing business. Win Investing LLP educates people on topics of trading and investing in the stock market and forex, so my new project would allow clients to copy experienced and profitable traders and place trades automatically when these traders did.

I decided to raise some money from investors and designed a presentation. I was so fired up and passionate about the project!

My business plan added up to a billion in the first three years, based on engaging just 2% of our 500,000 client database.

The business model was very logical and straightforward, which was why it was so easy to present to investors. I believed in the project so much and was so passionate about it that investors also got very fired up and were happy to offer hundreds of thousands of pounds based on trust. I also found Fintech expos, where venture capitalists would come to look for investment opportunities. So I created a presentation and decided to ask for £2 million from investors, even though I budgeted £500,000 to get the project up and running and to become profitable.

I booked a time-slot to present my project and was seated at a roundtable with investors and watched other people pitch their business ideas. It was a very interesting experience for me, and I learnt a lot from it.

At the end of my presentation, I had investors coming to me and saying that they really enjoyed the project and presentation but unfortunately their investments started from £5 million, and the amount I asked for was too small; therefore, they could not help me. I also had investors saying to me they would be happy funding such a small amount from their own pocket, so we could work something out.

I found a company of programmers that specialised in these matters. They developed an online banking system for a few banks in Russia and Estonia, so I thought they would be a perfect company for the job. We got started with enthusiasm, developed a plan, I made a first payment, and they did one month's worth of programming. Then regulations changed, so we had to get a fund manager licence. To get that would require passing exams, learning laws and regulations, and getting a compliance officer and sticking to bureaucratic rules, and I was not prepared to do it because it was not my 'true passion'.

Was it a stumbling block in my mind and beliefs that I was not prepared to do something that was needed in order to become a billionaire? Did I see obstacles rather than opportunities? I guess I did.

The interesting part is when I contacted investors and told them that the project was a no-go, they were quite upset and were not in any rush to get their money back. It took some explaining as to why we didn't want to carry on with the project. But after some back and forth emails, they regretfully sent me their bank details for their funds to be returned.

Why you should always do what you love

At some stage in my life, I didn't know what to do with myself. Now, because I have a different mindset, I don't feel I have to do anything.

I don't need to chase achievement or money.

I never have to do anything I don't want to do.

People often say to me, "Well, Tatjana, how come you don't invest in this? Or try setting up a business around that? You can make more money. Or why do you teach trading and don't just sit at home and trade?"

I simply do what and when I want to.

I know I can make more money from pretty much anything.

If someone wants help to start a business, and they don't know what to do, I can give them hundreds of ideas or advice. In fact I used to do that and it was one of my businesses – helping people to start and grow a company. I used to charge £5000 a day for that service and I had many happy clients. I have no shortage of creativity. I'm not trying to grab all the money in the world.

I want my money to come to me in an easy, fun, and pleasurable way – and I believe that I can help other people do the same.

I don't do things anymore because I have to. I don't do things because they're good for business or good for someone else.

That is why I decided to work on this book. Instead of getting bored, I'm entertaining myself, and I'm doing things because I like to and things producing value.

I feel a great need to share my journey and discovery of the power of ITT.

In turn, I aim to help you become more successful and happier and, through this book, I'm confident you can achieve this, too.

How to never work a day in your life

If you could get paid for your hobbies, how more wonderful would your life be?

Think about that. If you could just do a few things for the rest of your life and not worry about money, what would you do? I'm about to show you that doing what you love is the best way to serve others and the world.

Many people try to serve the world in a not very truthful way. A way that does themselves harm. They believe they have to work in a job they don't like or do something which doesn't fulfil them because they need the money to achieve their goals or support their family. They put others' needs before their own.

Question is: why not meet your obligations and look after your family by doing something you love that makes you happy?

Why do it all the wrong way round?

The true definition of help is when you are totally fulfilled in yourself, and you have the time, resources, and desire to help someone, if and when they come to you and ask for help.

The underlying belief in helping someone who has not asked for help is that there is something wrong with the person like they're not coping well, or they're weak or hopeless and can't do it themselves.

Quite often, it's a trap for people who do not want to focus on their own lives and issues. Instead, they try to focus on somebody else's problems.

Or they spend all their life trying to find their 'purpose' or focusing on what they 'should' be doing.

Recently, I've had people come to me, who want to find out their divine purpose, why they are here, and what their true calling is in life. People get so focused on what they are supposed to do, rather than enjoying their life. What's the point of any game? Is it to have fun and enjoy playing it, or is it to win? It is the first one because if you are trying to win, it is not a game anymore, it is a competition.

You can only do your best in a pleasant way when you actually love something that you do and enjoy doing it. If everyone in our society did what they loved, we'd have better healthcare, schools, restaurants, everything! When food is prepared with love, it tastes better. When teachers are passionate about their subject, their students learn more.

Instead of focusing on what you 'should' do or on what God thinks you should do, take responsibility for your life. Do something you are passionate about. It doesn't have to be for the rest of your life – passions change over time, but do something you love and enjoy.

When I teach seminars, I ask people what is their true passion, they come up with examples like: I want to save the world, I want to help people … I would tell them: not true. It sounds more like someone told them that it would be an honourable thing to do and therefore it is more of an obligation than true passion. But when they say: "I love dancing," "I love singing," or "I love teaching seminars," it's a completely different game, and there is truth in it and it's more about them, rather than what they think they should be doing.

If you take the right approach and apply some strategies I suggest, doing what you love can result in the financial rewards as a positive side effect, if you allow it to happen.

Sometimes people have strong limiting beliefs about getting paid for your passion. I worked with a lady who had an interesting belief, that said: as soon as she started doing what she loved for money, she would get bored. This lady loves travelling, but when she does it for too long – her last trip was six months – she doesn't want to do it anymore. When I asked her why she never finished her trip and fell out of love with it, she didn't have an answer. Her belief was more about lack of flexibility and freedom in changing her plans, if she was getting paid for doing what she loved – it just didn't occur to her.

What are your beliefs about making money from your hobbies? Is it possible for you?

If you live according to your highest potential and truth of The Creator, your life will be wonderful. You never have to work a single day in your life; when you do things you would do for free anyway, and you enjoy it, you cannot call it work.

You may have a scary big goal to earn millions from investing, trading, or business. I mean, it's not really that difficult to do. It's not rocket science, especially when you know how to use your intuition to help your trading. If you remove the element of self-sabotage and fear of big money, you will achieve your goals fast.

Exercise – Making money through my passion

Let's figure out what fulfils you, so we can work out what you can do to make money while having fun.

Write down at least three things that you absolutely love doing and you could do all day long, even if you didn't get paid for it.

It can be absolutely anything as long as it's something you like doing.

Even if it's things like eating or surfing the internet, these are allowed. You can make money from eating if you're a restaurant or food critic or a blogger who gets paid for going to the best restaurants in the world from sponsorships and product sales, given you have big enough number of followers.

Buying and selling is a lovely hobby. You can make money by trading on eBay, trading shares, or trading houses.

Teaching is a wonderful kind of fun, learning different things and meeting fantastic people.

If you put on your list that your passion is networking, organising events or being an influencer, I can give you a business idea right away. I can offer you to be my event organiser or an affiliate. The best way to sell a product or service is if you experienced it, got inspired and have faith in it. If you get big enough group of people, I would be happy to come and teach a seminar to them and you would be getting a cut of the revenue. I love doing talks for large audiences to have a bigger impact and influence the world for a positive change.

For everything you can think of, there is a way of making money from it, even if you don't have any money to begin with.

It is a beautiful thing that money makes money. If you say that you either don't have a lot of money or any money, remember, it doesn't have to be your money. It's possible to start a business or buy a property with other people's money if you know how.

In fact, you can start ANY business without any money whatsoever or without any investment. You can get financing or financial help from other people, and it doesn't even have to be people you know. Especially now in our internet and technology times.

I started my business without any funding – except maybe a fax machine! I just used my confidence and trust that everything would work out for me. I did everything that way without a second thought.

I know what it feels like to be creative in my business and how to find and attract the right team and the right customer. When you start a business, you will need to learn many things and develop a lot of virtues.

Now, I'm in a position to follow all my passions. My latest passion that I've turned into profit is jewellery and clothing design, which lights me up and allows me to be creative. To look at my latest designs and products, go here: www.prosperitycode.co.uk.

You can see how happy it makes me!

I do believe money is very "spiritual" because to make a lot of money you need to be creative enough and have the ability to manifest a lot.

So let's get on with making you more money.

Make money effortlessly ... in just one hour (Investing)

Trading is a great way to make money and can be a lot of fun.

You may not know how to make money from trading right now, yet it is simple and straightforward. All you need to do is master the right strategies.

This isn't a book on trading. What I could tell you about trading is probably another book in itself. I want to highlight to you here that trading doesn't need to be complicated or scary. You don't need to have a desk with eight monitors and stare at screens all day. It doesn't have to be like that at all.

As a senior coach in my investment training company – www.wininvesting.online – I teach advanced techniques for generating wealth. I am also now a fund manager and manage clients' money for them, if they don't want to spend time learning trading or time trading themselves. This was my latest project whilst I was writing this book. It just happened effortlessly and client just started giving me lots of money to make investments on their behalf.

You know, by now, that I like things to be fun, easy, and enjoyable – and that applies to my trading strategies. (You're not going to find any of the strategies that I teach in a textbook or stuffy old book on trading!)

When it comes to investing, working less is the answer to making more money than you can ever imagine.

For example, in one session, I show students how to follow a strategy that only takes an hour a year and consistently makes 100% return year-on-year. Can you spare one hour a year? Sure, you can!

It's all about knowing how to find the right companies and shares and then knowing what to do with them. Would you like 100% return a year for an hour's work?

There's another strategy I have called 'The Lunchtime Strategy'.

It does exactly what it says. It's made for people who are super-busy and don't have any time. And all you need to do is make a few trades while you eat. You trade during lunchtime or dinner, find the trade, get in and out within few minutes or so with a few % return. How easy does that sound? And it works!

When people tell you making money is hard and trading is difficult or risky, they show up their own beliefs about money. You can choose to be free of these beliefs and realise making money can be as effortless and fun as you want it to be. I should know – these strategies prove it!

If you want to discover more about trading mastery and how to spend less time making more money, download our guide to wealth at www.wininvesting.com or sign up for financial and economic updates at www.darrenwinters.com

How to use everything you've already got to make money

There's always one significant objection I hear from people who haven't gone through this process:

"How do I get started when I don't have any money or resources?"

You know now that we live in abundance, and you have resources all around you. You can access these freely and at will. But this exercise will help you start seeing how resourceful you are.

Once you're clear on what you want and what you like to do, the next thing is to make a list of all your resources. This is a really good exercise even if you're already in business (you may surprise yourself!).

Exercise – Your money-making resources

We're going to write another list. (I hope you love writing lists by now!) This is going to be a great list of all the resources you have to make money, grow wealth, or build a business.

Write down what ideas you have to improve your situation or take your business to the next level. Put on the list absolutely anything that comes to mind, like any recommendation or useful website, seminars that can help you learn and even this book you're reading! If you want to help your friend to get out of a difficult situation, you could give this book to them!

You can get advice from any professionals in your circle. This may include tax advisors, accountants, marketing people, lawyers, and salespeople. Anyone you know who has a skill you may need in your business is a resource you can possibly access, too.

Then write down any business gurus or money gurus you can learn from and find out more about. These days you can get all the information you need. Today, the problem isn't a lack of information. The problem is too much information. It's overwhelming. And it can be challenging to discern what is useful information and what is not or even harmful. There is a lot of misleading advice because anyone can say they are an expert.

Here's where you can use your newfound knowledge.

Now you have superior awareness you can ask The Creator how suitable the experience of any person is for you. You can also ask if a particular book, article, or resource is worth reading or has value you can use to improve your situation. You can also manifest the right sources of information and for the right people to come your way. Use your intuition to attract the right partners into your business.

Remember, other people can also be your resources for a particular project or business.

Look, I can already think of one person who can be your mentor and be on your team: Tatjana Valujeva – Prosperity Coach!

How one free ad made me £7000

When I started my business in 1994, Facebook didn't exist (Mark Zuckerberg barely existed!).

To get business, I tried all the obvious opportunities – business networking, speed networking, everything. I even posted an advert on a supermarket board, back then, when I lived in Beckton.

There was a supermarket that had a board for local people to advertise their services, so I posted a free stock market course.

That one little free advert brought me at least one customer (they told me when they registered that there is where they found me). That one customer went on to pay £2000 for a course and then a further £5000 for advanced strategies Masterclass – that £7000 from this one supermarket post.

Most people would have dismissed that little ad, but I always see an opportunity for me. There are possibilities everywhere to find your perfect customer.

How to get others to help you build your business

I was in St Petersburg recently on a business trip.

While I was there, a lady approached me, asking if I would run my *Money Magic* course for her. Now, I wasn't on Facebook at the time, and I certainly wasn't promoting my course. Everyone who has attended my *Money Magic* course to this point has found me in much the same fortuitous way I found the healers and courses that I attended.

So that was the first thing.

She told me she had heard about me and was planning to travel to London to do the course. But now I was in St Petersburg, where she lived, she really wanted me to do it there.

She asked me, "How many people do you need to run the course?"

"Six," I said. She managed to get six people together to run the course in 24 hours. Now, that's motivation!

The course was a lot of fun with six highly motivated students, and it didn't end there. Next, they all wanted me to teach them the instructor course, which is more expensive but allows them to go out and teach my course within Russia.

Here's the really interesting part, which shows the importance of thinking ahead. They'll go out and teach and will show the system to probably around 100 people. Those 100 people will most likely then want to become instructors, and so I can go and teach them.

By showing others how to teach, they create the market for me.

This is something you can do as well.

Think how you can do something once and get your customers to keep building your business for you.

How to dominate your market by making this one little change

Jay Abraham is an amazing expert. I've already spoken about how I spent a lot of money and time with Jay in coaching, and it was a fantastic experience.

He teaches you to value yourself, your time, and your product, and how to build faith and trust in your product from a customer perspective.

When you are starting in business for the first time, it can be hard to get customers. Jay has a powerful suggestion that can propel your business to the top.

His recommendation is to offer a money-back guarantee if your customer is not happy for any reason whatsoever. He even suggests a double money-back guarantee, where you pay them back more if they're not satisfied.

Some companies around are so confident in their product they are happy to offer a guarantee like this. And that's exactly why doing this will help you stand out from everyone else in your market.

It shows a tremendous amount of faith in your product, and that's the reason it works so well.

If that seems a bit scary (and it will at first), it doesn't need to be an unconditional guarantee. You can put conditions in that people have to use your product and show that they've used it. The reality is, the majority of people who buy any product don't use it – or don't use it properly.

This guarantee works for everything, whether you're selling £2000 courses or T-shirts. If people are not happy for any reason, they can return it.

OK, OK, I know what you're going to ask next:

"But, Tatjana, what if I get a lot of refunds?!"

If you get a wave of refunds, that's a GOOD thing. Yes, it is! It may be because something is wrong with your product (which you definitely want to know), or your service or product isn't up to scratch, and you need to make it better (which is always a good thing).

Let's put things in perspective. I offer a guarantee, and since 1999 in financial training business, offering that guarantee has attracted tens of thousands of clients. And in that time I've only had to refund five clients ever!

It is SO irrelevant to the whole picture of your finances that it shouldn't be a problem. It creates SO much value and much more interest in your product!

Learn to say "I don't know" (and delegate!)

Some people find it very difficult to accept they don't know something. VERY difficult.

In fact, they'll even start talking nonsense to show they are knowledgeable. It's so obvious they have no clue.

I'm sure there's someone you know that's just like this. Or you can think of many situations when this has happened.

The crazy thing is, when you try to cover up your ignorance, you do the opposite: you look even more stupid. By saying, "I don't know," you show more confidence. You appear more in control, more successful, and confident when you don't have to prove anything.

Learn to be honest and say:

"I don't know; I will find out and get back to you,"

or

"This will be interesting to explore."

There's nothing wrong with not knowing everything. You're not expected to know everything on this planet.

Ask yourself, do you really need to learn all those skills? Or do you just need to focus on what you are very good at and trust someone else to do the other jobs? This doesn't mean you're putting the responsibility onto them; you are delegating.

There is a difference between delegating and handing off responsibility. If you're a business owner, and your accountant makes an error, ultimately, you are still the one responsible.

Your staff come and go in your business, people come and go in your life. You remain, so you still need to have an understanding of accounts, tax, and other elements that are essential for running your business and managing your wealth. You don't have to be manually doing it, but having some basic knowledge is a good idea.

Seriously, knowing how to build a team of talents is one part of the success formula worth learning sooner rather than later. Which leads us nicely onto Robert Kiyosaki's advice on building a 'dream team'.

The power of the team

Robert Kiyosaki, author of *Rich Dad, Poor Dad* is one of the world's greatest wealth gurus. We were privileged to share the stage with Robert and meet with him in person.

At one event, I asked Robert what the secret of his success was. Rather than a particular wealth strategy or hack, his answer surprised me.

He told me that the secret of his success was his team. I call this the 'dream team', and your dream team will help you take your business to the next level.

If you don't know something or if you don't have a particular skill, somebody else in the world will. There will always be someone who knows how to do something you don't or do something you don't want to do. The person will actually love doing the thing you can't or don't want to do and will achieve far better results than you in that field.

Removing the belief that only you can do everything better will finally allow you to focus and concentrate on something that you love doing. That is the power of delegation.

It's essential to be efficient in communication, collaboration, and interaction in your business, so you respect yourself and have healthy relationships with your colleagues.

With the right team, you will always feel able to speak your truth, your opinions, and do so confidently, calmly, and peacefully. With some practise, you will be able to do so with anyone.

As Kiyosaki explains it, rich people don't work for money; rich people work to own resources. There is always primary and secondary wealth. Our primary wealth is resource, and our secondary wealth is production. Money is not usually one or the other. Money is an end result of owning resources or production.

With a business and the right team, you have a fantastic opportunity and the ability to help people and create value.

How to stand out (according to Richard Branson)

Of course, the master of the publicity stunts is billionaire Richard Branson.

Branson has launched and grown several billion-pound businesses, selling everything from flights to cola, weddings to gym memberships. Alongside his huge successes, he's also had some high profile 'failures' (although I'm sure he doesn't see it that way – and nor should you!). But what really shines through from Branson is his undimmed enthusiasm and determination.

He knows the power of using a personal brand to launch any business and secrets of PR for brand building.

Branson is well-known for creating good PR and personally doing a lot of the publicity stunts in his business. You need to establish a name for yourself as an expert in your niche. Even if you do something slightly scandalous, it can be in a positive way (however, it should never cause harm to people).

You can succeed in viral marketing by doing exciting and outrageous stunts that will have the desired effect on the business and attract the attention of your target audience.

Here's another interesting thing about Branson's PR stunts. Many of those – like swimming across the ocean, flying in a balloon, and all the parachute jumps – aren't just for publicity. They are for his own fun and personal achievement. Branson truly understands how doing what you love fulfils you while making money.

Another element that helps Branson's businesses stand out is his willingness to do things that nobody else has done before. He is the master when it comes to launching completely new concepts. Virgin Galactic will soon start trips into space, and I'm sure it will be very successful, despite some challenges.

But what he did with Virgin Atlantic was ground-breaking and, in the process, changed the whole market for air travel. The story of the Virgin Atlantic and British Airways battle has been well-documented, but it's worth repeating how Branson's determination to do things that matter changed all our lives.

He took all the biggest airlines in the world to court to break the monopoly over routes. The battle stretched his resources to its limits and cost millions of pounds. But he actually managed to win, and the result was freedom for new companies to come into the market and drive prices down, like EasyJet and Ryanair. Flights which used to cost £400–£500, you could now buy for £15. It was a victory for consumers. If anyone proves the value of helping others, it is Branson.

By the way, this doesn't mean he takes unnecessary risks. One trait that separates the wealthy from everyone else is their approach to risk. According to Branson, the ratio of risk to reward should be at least two to one or more. It is not worth taking completely unnecessary and unjustified gambles.

Want to discover even more of Branson's wealth secrets? Join the *Money Magic* workshop to learn more about wealth gurus such as Richard Branson, Robert Kiyosaki, and Brian Tracy. For more details, go to www.prosperitycode.co.uk.

Get attention by stealing puppies (or how to stand out on social media)

You either love marketing, or you don't. When you love what you do, though, it doesn't feel like marketing.

When it comes to getting attention, social media, of course, is a fantastic opportunity at the moment.

You can always find your ideal clients and try to turn them into followers, as long as you know how to create valuable content.

(Honest truth from me, here – I don't like spending my time on marketing. It's not my area of expertise, so I hire someone to do it for me, but it's worth it.)

The key to getting more exposure on social media is making your content go viral. How do you make it go viral and stand out from everything else?

Well, it isn't predictable because you need to be in tune with what is trending. A good approach is to be bold and experiment. Find out what everyone else is doing in your market – and then improve on it!

The crazier, bolder, and more eye-catching, the better. You have to be very creative to get attention now.

One speaker I know does a lot of YouTube videos. He tests all kinds of funny things to get attention and persuade his viewers to share his content. For people to share your videos, they need to be funny, controversial, useful, or emotional (fun, shock, passion, love, sadness, fear, pain and pleasure).

He once did a video when he was super-friendly and went out speaking to people in the street. In his friendliness, he put his arm around one woman who ended up reporting him to the police for sexual harassment!

It's hilarious (although not for the poor woman) as he ended up getting arrested, but the video went viral, and he got a few million hits.

(All publicity is good publicity, right?)

Another crazy stunt he tried was kidnapping a dog – his own dog. As you know, Britain is a country of dog lovers, so he did something that would really get attention.

He filmed a short video, which looked like an attempted dog theft. He asked a friend to walk his dog and made it look like he was stalking it. Obviously, the viewers didn't realise, and it went viral. He always made sure he did something funny at the end of the video, so viewers would be encouraged to attend his webinars.

There are millions of ways to make things exciting and watchable. You have the resources, and now the Internet is at your disposal, so you can experiment. You just need to be creative.

How to get on TV (or get ANY free publicity)

When I'm speaking at events to students and people who have never met me before, I start my presentation with a clip from a TV channel, *Women in the Property Market*.

The clip is from an interview between me and the presenters, where I'm talking about the success I've had in the property market. Getting on TV that time was great for my profile and helped me build trust really quickly with people who didn't know me. And it all came about because I had to be resourceful.

You see, right at the start of my career, I didn't have any money to invest in advertising. I had to find a source of free business and free leads. (Sometimes having no money can also be beneficial in some instances.)

I did what I recommend at seminars that everyone should create publicity by giving value to people and sharing their expertise. That helps you become a renowned expert fast.

If someone writes a weekly column for a newspaper or magazine, they automatically become known to their readers. Think how you could benefit and how readers could benefit from your content in articles, magazines, or even TV or radio.

Believe me, good content is always a struggle for TV companies and many publications. These publications usually use some kind of filler when they're short of good content. They desperately need interesting topics, new experts on different subjects, and something that will impress or surprise the readers – especially if it's free!

If you can suggest a topic that appeals to their viewers or readers, many channels will be happy to have you on the programme.

That's precisely how I ended up on *Women in the Property Market*. Someone from the TV channel met me on a seminar and asked me if I would agree to take a half-hour slot on the TV programme as they wanted to have more women who invested in property.

They sent a limo to pick me up, and when I arrived at the studio, I met my own make-up artist. Two ladies that hosted the programme told me not to worry about mistakes as it was their job, as presenters, to keep everything on track. As a guest, I was allowed to say whatever I wanted.

Another great place to look is speaking opportunities at events and getting slots at trade shows or exhibitions.

Not many people like speaking (public speaking is one of the biggest fears for people in the UK!), but nearly every event needs fillers and content. Think like the organiser – they want the audience to walk away feeling like it's a great event with great content. You just have to show them you can help them achieve that.

This was great publicity for me. And it will work for you, too.

The equation for your first million

Right at the start of this section, I told you I'd reveal the formula for making your first million.

By now, I hope you see why it was necessary to go on a journey. So many books try to show you how to make money through business, trading, property, or whatever. The reason they don't work for everyone and all the time is they don't take into consideration the uniqueness of each person and the intricate details of the person's psychology and belief system. Now you see through our time together, how these pieces fit together.

So, here's the equation:

Your dream + your passion – limiting beliefs + virtues + your team + unconditional love

Write this down. Hang it above your desk or wherever you're going to see it most. Manifest and take action. If you ever get stuck, check what's missing in your life out of this formula.

Hopefully, you've done all the exercises to this point. As you can see, each one builds on the other to give you everything you need in this equation.

First, you decided what your goals were and what you actually wanted. Now, you just need to choose the ideas you want to implement and get moving on them and turn it into a business.

When you follow your passions, making money doesn't feel like work. Think what your true passion is – that you can monetise – so you can become prosperous and fulfilled.

I meet more and more people like that these days, people who have made their money and realise they can serve the planet.

The goal of the *The Prosperity Code* is to create value and enrich the lives of others while enriching ourselves. No sacrifices, no hardships or struggles. It's a win–win situation for everyone. If you enjoyed my ideas and strategies and you felt it inspired you, pay it forward and help your loved ones by giving them a copy of this book.

The purpose of every business is to improve the quality of our lives. If you look around now, see that everything – a chair, a sofa, a computer, a pen, paper – everything earned money for the business owner, who made it. Everything can bring you money.

Don't ever be discouraged if somebody else tells you, "Oh, that's a silly idea, that will never work." If other people don't understand your idea, it's not your problem it's theirs. As long as you have an idea, and you have a passion for it, there's no reason why it won't work.

Act on it, and the reward will come. You can do this.

Now it's your turn to play The Game

You've learned some essential lessons about wealth, and I've given you everything you need to start playing The Game ... and win!

No matter what way you choose to make money and build wealth, with these principles, you can succeed.

What's more, it's easy, simple, and fun doing something you love. It doesn't feel like work. And when it doesn't feel like work, you can always be happy.

Think like those millionaires who love going to work every day, because it's fun. And remember, if I can do it, so can you!

But I'm not letting you off the hook. I want to know what you're doing. I want to hear how you're going to make your first million! I don't want you to put this book down or do anything else until you've done this:

Pull out your phone or open your computer and send me a message right now. Tell me about your dreams and business ideas. Also, if you look for investors, send me your business plan, and you might even get me or some of my contacts interested.

Seriously, I want to hear what you're going to do.

Let me know at tania@prosperitycode.co.uk

Now you know ... you have no excuse, right?

The surprising message from far, far away

It's strange how things work out.

In fact, you wouldn't be reading this book right now if it wasn't for a chance encounter with a lady from a small village in Russia ten hours away on the other side of the world.

This girl, Nadia, is the person I referenced in my acknowledgements at the start of this book because she's part of the reason this book exists. And it's such a strange story.

One day I was just on my computer when a contact request popped up on Skype. It was this girl who asked me to add her and then asked me to scan some problem she had.

She was only 19, and she had Googled me – difficult at the time because I wasn't interested in being found – and she decided I had the moral right to talk about money. So she contacted me, asked to be scanned and then told me to write a course about money, so she could promote it.

Well, at the time, I wasn't really interested in money as a topic, because I'd done so many financial courses at that moment in my life. But she was talking about money from a holistic perspective.

I sat down to meditate on this at midnight, and it was amazing because the information started coming to me as I was tuned into this idea. I wrote the whole course in 40 minutes!

I spoke to Nadia the next day and said I had written the course and she asked if she could promote it in Russia. She managed to get 100 people on that first course. At the time, she could only send money via Western Union, and so I would get cash three times a day she was selling so many courses. She was a social media genius, and she knew how to sell.

I wrote other courses for her to promote – a five-day course and a short half-day course – and sold these.

And then Nadia just disappeared. She was so talented and a very good writer, but then all of a sudden she deleted all her pages, left Skype, and I never heard from her again. But I'll never forget the impact she had at the time, which is why she is one of the people I want to say thank you to.

How to change the world, one book at a time

Thank you for reading this book. I can't tell you how delighted I am that you've spent this time with me and allowed me to guide you on the path to living an easy, fun, and enjoyable life.

It is my wish that you have taken many valuable teachings from this book that you can use in your life right away.

Helping yourself is the first step. And helping others who have been in your situation is the next.

And that's why I would like to ask you that if you know of anyone – a friend, family member or colleague – who struggles with money or other life issues and is held back by beliefs that don't serve them, please share the message this book carries.

I love to hear stories of how my readers have purchased another copy of the book (or two, three, or even more copies!) to give to those who they know need guidance and how it changed their life.

(Maybe you've been given this book by a friend who read it before.)

If this book has been of value to you, and you know someone who would benefit from reading it, please pass it on. A gift of a book that changes someone's trajectory will cause ripples of positivity into the future, a 'butterfly effect'.

Here's a chance to quickly, easily, and simply impact someone else's life – just by gifting this book!

When you do gift a book to someone who needs it, please head over to my Facebook page here – https://www.facebook.com/ProsperExpert/ – and tag me so I can see your good deed.

*"You will see magic,
when you look for it"*

TATJANA VALUJEVA

What next?

You're ready to go and change your world.

In the time we've spent together, I've shown you a method to uncreate your limiting and damaging beliefs. These beliefs have held you back from the abundance you deserve.

No more.

By adding some resources and virtues, you now have the tools to go and create wealth and live a more fulfilled life as an 'Enlightened Millionaire'.

By now, I hope you see there is a better way to live your life – a way that is simple, easy and fun.

It doesn't have to be a struggle. It doesn't have to be hard. Abundance flows freely and effortlessly to you.

You can make money and create wealth doing what you love, and that energises you. Now, I've shown you the way, you can begin using this in your life today.

So, what next?

Well, there are a few ways to continue our journey together:

1. Follow me on Facebook at www.facebook.com/ ProsperExpert

Here, I share more *Prosperity Code* secrets to clear beliefs that don't serve you and manifest your abundance. I show you how to use ITT in every part of your life. I also offer downloads to help achieve your goals fast.

2. Join the email list at www.prosperitycode.co.uk

Some tips I share are too much for Facebook! The deep secrets I reserve for subscribers to my mailing list. Join today and stay in the loop for my very best advice.

3. Join the next Money Magic programme

Get the full programme on how to create wealth. Together we'll work on all the lessons covered in this book to create your new reality. Discover more about the full programme here www.prosperitycode.co.uk .

So, now it's over to you. What are you going to do with all this knowledge, how much wealth you can create in your life, how much more fun, joy, prosperity, abundance, compassion and love you can give and receive?

Seriously, why are you still here?
Go!

Money Magic workshop

Money Magic will reprogram your brain and rewire your neuron connections for prosperity and success.

This event will give you clear understanding on process of money creation.

You will learn how money is made without ever working again.

You will get a clear vision of how money and abundance can come to you from different sources.

You will discover new ways of getting money and abundance.

You will learn multiple ways of removing virus programs and beliefs, which slow down your financial abundance and prosperity

Find out wealth secrets of Robert Kiyosaki, Richard Branson, Brian Tracy, Jay Abraham and myself, which I did not share in this book.

Get the much need resources for anything you want in life instantly (for wealth, health, career or relationships)

Enrich your knowledge bank with solid strategies on how to safeguard your assets, investments, comfort and stability.

You might also meet possible investors, who will be ready to fund your business and be valuable partners for developing your ideas.

Learn technique for accessing a circle of venture capitalists, who might be interested to invest from £5 million or more.

And most importantly – understand yourself and what was blocking your way to even bigger success, what stopped you from getting desired results, get rid of procrastination, blocks, prejudices, fears and any excuses, why things did not work out for you.

How to connect with your intuition and start trusting yourself.

Manifesting techniques to get whatever you desire instantly.

It's All About Your Money:
Learn About It. Create It. Have It. Enjoy it.

Is it possible to earn your first million, even though you don't have enough income or savings at the moment? Absolutely!

Tatjana Valujeva, author of *The Prosperity Code* and millionaire herself, shares her secrets and gives practical techniques on money-making with fast, effective and guaranteed results.

The *Money Magic* programme is a unique opportunity for everyone who aims at a wealthy and successful life and is ready to turn investment in this knowledge into growing abundance of money, confidence, love, and a happy future.

We are born to live a wealthy and happy life. However, not everyone is ready to accept the destined money flows, even knowing that it could improve his or her lifestyle in a radical way.

This course will help you attract more abundance into your life, increase your awareness, and make the best use out of them. You will get priceless knowledge, which will let you get as much money as you want to live the way you have always dreamt about.

In *Money Magic*, you will discover:

- What is money? What does it mean for you?
- Learning about money energy; new perception of money; setting positive beliefs.
- Personal 'money map' recreation, successful money manifestation and ways to earn more money
- Manifestation practice and practical exercises
- Releasing blocks against effective manifestations
- Rules and energy of money.
- How to make manifestation work.
- How to live in the moment and have harmony with money, earn by doing things you like and making money work for you.

Course duration: 2 days

Format: 4 webinars – 2 hours each.

Dates: once each group is formed.

*Theta-healing practitioners, as well as people working with other energy practices, are more than welcome to join. *Money Magic* also presents some of the most effective techniques that anyone can practice easily.

Register for the next course at www.prosperitycode.co.uk today.

CPSIA information can be obtained
at www.ICGtesting.com
Printed in the USA
BVHW090852010721
610973BV00025B/957

9 781913 962586